The Marketing Game!
with Student CD-Rom

Third Edition

Charlotte H. Mason
Kenan-Flagler Business School
University of North Carolina at Chapel Hill

William D. Perreault, Jr.
Kenan-Flagler Business School
University of North Carolina at Chapel Hill

McGraw-Hill
Irwin

Boston   Burr Ridge, IL   Dubuque, IA   Madison, WI   New York   San Francisco   St. Louis
Bangkok   Bogotá   Caracas   Kuala Lumpur   Lisbon   London   Madrid   Mexico City
Milan   Montreal   New Delhi   Santiago   Seoul   Singapore   Sydney   Taipei   Toronto

McGraw-Hill Higher Education

A Division of The McGraw-Hill Companies

The Marketing Game with Student CD-Rom
Charlotte H. Mason and William D. Perreault, Jr.

Published by McGraw-Hill/Irwin, an imprint of the McGraw-Hill Companies, Inc., 1221 Avenue of the Americas, New York, NY 10020. Copyright © 2002, 1995, 1992 by Charlotte H. Mason and William D. Perreault, Jr. All rights reserved.

13 14 CUS CUS 0 9

ISBN 9780256139884
MHID 0256139881

www.mhhe.com

About the Authors

CHARLOTTE H. MASON

Charlotte Mason is Associate Professor of Marketing at the Kenan-Flagler Business School, University of North Carolina at Chapel Hill. She received her Ph.D. from Stanford University in 1985. Dr. Mason's research specialization is the development of marketing models. In fact, *The Marketing Game!* simulation builds on her research in modeling the demand for new products. Her publications include articles in Journal of Consumer Research, Marketing Science, Journal of Marketing Research, and Marketing Letters. She also serves on the editorial review boards of several major journals, including the Journal of Marketing Research and Journal of Marketing. Prior to her academic career, Dr. Mason worked at Procter & Gamble—where her major responsibilities focused on designing and programming simulations used in strategic planning. Following that experience, she worked as a consultant for Booz Allen—where she was also involved in developing simulations for Booz Allen's clients.

WILLIAM D. PERREAULT, Jr.

William D. Perreault, Jr. is Kenan Professor at the Kenan-Flagler Business School, University of North Carolina at Chapel Hill. His contributions to the field of marketing have been recognized with both the American Marketing Association's Distinguished Educator Award and the Academy of Marketing Science's Outstanding Educator Award. He has served as the editor of the Journal of Marketing Research and on the editorial review board for a number of other journals. He is coauthor, with E. J. McCarthy, of two other widely used marketing texts—Basic Marketing and Essentials of Marketing. Dr. Perreault has been developing and working with marketing simulations for 25 years—both in the classroom and in industry.

Preface

We are excited about this new third edition of *The Marketing Game!* And we hope you will be too. It includes many new innovations and improvements that build on the success of our earlier simulation, and it incorporates the latest thinking in the field.

At the risk of "getting ahead of ourselves," we'll give you a quick preview of what's new with this edition. We have completely redesigned and reprogrammed all of the software. The new Windows software that accompanies the student manual is easy to use, offers context-specific help, and makes it even easier to submit marketing plan decisions and print reports. The new instructor software has an innovative design that saves time—making it fast and easy for instructors to setup and run the simulation, even when dealing with a large number of competing firms. For example, the instructor software now automatically checks that relevant plan and history files for all firms (regardless of the number of industries) are available, and then a "single click" runs the simulation and prepares reports for all industries in "batch" mode according to options set by the instructor. The software provides both instructor and student users with on-screen "hints"—and the comprehensive online help system addresses any questions that may arise.

The software now creates password-protected plans and (at the instructor's option) Report files; this system relies on advanced 128-bit encryption technologies for added security. This provides an easy and secure way for faculty and students to take advantage of advances in information technology and exchange plan and results files electronically—whether from an Internet website, by email, over a school's network, or even via an FTP server.

We've also designed the structure of computer files so that they are resistant to destructive computer viruses. This is a nontrivial consideration in today's university computing environments. *The Marketing Game!* protects both faculty and students from risks and damage of viruses that plague use of many other simulations, especially those that have been built by simply overlaying "macros" on existing software (such as Excel spreadsheet templates).

The analytical foundation for the underlying simulation model has been updated and "tuned" to make the pedagogical experience even more effective. And, of course, the case materials presented in this book that provide the context of the marketing competition have been completely updated and refined to reflect innovations in the information technology arena. These teaching and learning enhancements are significant, but at the same time it is important to see that they build on the core principles that motivated earlier editions of the game.

Nearly 15 years ago we started work on the first edition of *The Marketing Game!* Our aspiration was not just to improve on other competitive marketing simulations that had been available in the past; rather, our goal was to pioneer a new generation of simulations. We wanted the game to be flexible, so it would effectively serve a wide variety of marketing teaching and learning needs, from the most basic to the most sophisticated. We wanted it to be the best simulation ever offered, and at the same time the easiest to use—so it would be attractive to people who had never previously considered teaching with a simulation. We wanted to design it to be rich in student interest and realism, and yet to create a strategy-planning environment where random events would not mask the relationship between good decisions and results achieved. No one learns anything in situations like that, but even today that is typical in most other marketing simulations. We also wanted participants both to have fun and be challenged analyzing the results of the simulation and planning new strategies. At the same time, we wanted to make it fast and easy for instructors to diagnose how participants were progressing. In sum, our wish list in preparing the first edition of the game appeared to represent a tall order!

It is indeed gratifying that the game has been an enduring success—and that students and instructors alike have been enthusiastic about what we achieved toward our original objectives. Nevertheless, over time, creative colleagues at hundreds of colleges, universities, and companies who had worked with the earlier editions of the game for a number of years came up with a host of great ideas on ways to make it even better. We took their shared suggestions, criticisms and ideas about ways to improve or update the student manual, the student and instructor software, the underlying simulation model, and the other instructor materials and made this edition even better. Our most ardent supporters and loyal users have often been our best critics!

When we created the game, it was the easiest to setup and use of any simulation. Now it is even easier. With this edition, our objective is to take advantage of the capabilities of the Windows operating system and the Internet to not only expand the flexibility and ease of use of our original design, but also to add new features that will make digital communications between instructors and students faster and more secure. We are quick to admit that it has taken longer than we anticipated to meet the standard we set … primarily because we started over again from scratch midway through the process of creating the new software. The reason is simple. When we started that process our focus was evolutionary—to simply convert the original software to be Windows compatible. However, our "wish list" for user benefits and vision for how to make that wish list a reality expanded as advances in technology created new opportunities. While the period of development and testing has taken longer than we anticipated, the results reflect the investment of time and effort that we made.

In the spirit of earlier editions, *The Marketing Game!* is designed to provide the basis for a high-involvement learning experience. It's fun. But it is also challenging. The focus is on effective marketing strategy planning in a competitive environment. It gives you the opportunity to analyze markets and target market needs. You make decisions in a number of strategy decision areas—to develop an integrated marketing plan that satisfies your target market and earns a profit for your firm. You can use the TMGPlan software that comes with this manual to more easily and quickly evaluate the budget and financial implications of your strategy; you can also view or print reports of the results achieved ... and there is no worry that someone else who doesn't have your password will have access to your proprietary marketing plans or reports.

It has been a priority to make the simulation—and the market environment— realistic. Firms compete by developing and marketing one or more products— and supporting customers with service after-the-sale. Marketing managers select and focus on target markets from among a variety of business and consumer segments—and reach their targets with different channels. Promotion—including personal selling, advertising and sales promotion—must consider middlemen and final customers. Prices must be set to offer customers the value they seek and yield profits for the firm. The simulation starts in the growth stage of the product life cycle—and continues into market maturity. R&D decisions make it possible to modify the product(s) over time to better meet customer needs and competitive challenges. The game can continue for as many decision periods as the instructor desires. The instructor also has a variety of optional ways to "setup" or adjust the market environment to meet specific teaching and learning objectives.

Both the text and computer simulation have been carefully written to build on the marketing strategy planning framework and the 4Ps organization pioneered by E. Jerome McCarthy. This organization is used in Basic Marketing—the most widely used text in marketing. But, importantly, it has been adopted and used in almost every other marketing text. Moreover, because this framework really works, it has become the cornerstone of marketing strategy planning in most firms. By building on this standard we ensure that the simulation will work well in a variety of learning and teaching situations—and with students who have different levels of knowledge and experience—whether the students are just learning about marketing or are seasoned executives.

In fact, this flexibility is possible because the game is not based on just one simulation, but several simulations within one integrated framework. It has been specially designed so that the instructor can select the number of decision areas—and if desired increase the number of decision areas (and thus the difficulty level) over time. This innovation, introduced with the first edition of the game, is one reason the game quickly became one of the most widely used marketing simulations in the world. It continues to be a comparative advantage of the game and why it works well whether it is used with senior executives in management development programs, with undergraduate and graduate students in the first marketing course, or with students in electives such as marketing strategy and product management.

One of the key advantages of using a simulation rather than some other realistic learning approach—such as case discussions or industry studies—is that it provides immediate feedback. Even in the real world feedback is often slow—and mistakes can certainly be very costly. In contrast, with a well-designed simulation, strategies can be formulated and then tested and refined over time. It is difficult for any other type of teaching or learning approach to give students an in-depth opportunity to develop plans, evaluate how their decisions are playing out in a competitive market, and then revise the strategy to seize opportunities and avoid threats. The experience and learning that result are cumulative.

We have designed *The Marketing Game!* to ensure that these pedagogical benefits are realized. It is set in a dynamic market environment. Thus, a poor decision early in the competition does not frustrate the learning process or leave a student/manager with poor results from then on. New decision periods bring opportunities for new successes. And firms with early successes can't coast on their laurels, but must constantly "earn" their customers' business. Thus, there is ample opportunity to learn from both successes and mistakes.

In addition, this is not a narrowly defined market in which success by one firm dooms others to failure. There are a number of different types of opportunities to pursue. Each firm can develop its own effective and profitable marketing strategy. As in the real world, the marketing manager in the game decides whether to compete head-on with other firms or pursue a segment or segments with less competition. Either way, however, good decisions produce good results. As simple as that sounds, it is perhaps the single greatest strength of this simulation—and where so many other simulations fall short.

Moreover, this is not a "zero sum" game—one in which one competitor must lose for another one to win. While many other simulations rely on the assumptions of zero sum competition, we believe that approach fails to consider the pedagogical reasons for using a simulation in the first place. It simply doesn't make sense to assume that if one student participant does a good job that another must be doing a bad job. In *The Marketing Game!* good work and smart decisions are reinforced with good outcomes—and that reinforces the learning process for everyone involved.

A marketing budget for each firm in each period highlights the trade-offs among marketing expenditures that marketing managers must make when developing a marketing strategy. A "smart" marketing strategy must be based on a marketing mix that is consistent with target market needs—but that doesn't mean that it must be a high-cost strategy.

The text includes budget planning and marketing strategy forms that help develop skills in analyzing alternative marketing plans. These forms can be used singly or in combination with the accompanying TMGPlan software, which is discussed in Appendix A at the end of this text.

There is a very complete, extensively revised and upgraded *Instructor's Manual to Accompany The Marketing Game!* It is available in both a print and (hyper linked) electronic version (with full text search). The manual gives many suggestions to help make the simulation a successful teaching/learning experience for instructors and students alike.

We have made hundreds of revisions and improvements in the simulation software, the instructor materials, and in this book. We won't catalog all of the changes here. After all, a long "what's new" list probably isn't relevant for most students who are participating in the game for the first time. But instructors who have used the game in the past will find a detailed list of the changes at the beginning of the revised instructor's manual. It also provides a set of "quick start" instructions that will be an aid for both experienced and new users.

Our students—and hundreds of our colleagues from around the world who teach with the game—report that *The Marketing Game!* is an exciting and integrating learning experience.

Our sincere hope is that you will have the same reaction.

Acknowledgments

Many people have made important contributions to *The Marketing Game!*

We owe the greatest debt to our students—in undergraduate, graduate, and executive program courses—who used "beta test" versions of this edition of *The Marketing Game!* Their enthusiasm about the experience—and what they were learning—was an important motivator for us. In addition, the thousands of marketing plans that they have submitted over the years have helped us to refine and improve the simulation. And their questions and suggestions gave us ideas on ways to improve the text.

We especially appreciate the many faculty—and the count is in the hundreds at this point—who have taken the time and initiative to write or call with detailed suggestions concerning *The Marketing Game!* Hopefully, these valued colleagues will see that we have taken their expert inputs seriously. The vast majority of the changes in this new edition were stimulated by the suggestions they provided.

We are grateful to our faculty colleagues and current and past doctoral candidates at the Kenan-Flagler Business School. They have been eager supporters of the game, and in our own "backyard" have demonstrated a wide variety of creative new ways to use the game. It's often said that "imitation is the sincerest form of flattery." So our colleagues should be flattered that many of their creative ideas and approaches are now incorporated in the game and supporting materials.

We are especially grateful to Melissa Martin. She has been a superb collaborator in administering the game and working with approximately 1000 students. She independently created the game website that served as the prototype for the web template now available with the instructor materials. And most important she has been an enormous help with programming the new version of the software. She tracked down and eliminated programming bugs and took responsibility for converting our 16-bit Windows software design to the final 32-bit form you will work with. We would have both pulled out our hair during this process if it were not for her initiative, attention to detail, persistence, and creativity.

During the past decade we have been invited to give many presentations and participate in a variety of workshops, consortia, conferences, and institutes concerning the use of simulations in marketing education. These events have spanned a number of countries, and included organizations ranging from the Marketing Education Group in the United Kingdom, American Marketing Association, Society for Marketing Advances, Western Marketing Association, and other professional societies in the U.S., as well as groups such as the American Assembly of Collegiate Schools of Business. We appreciate the opportunity to share our ideas at these gatherings and in presentations at a large number of universities. They have given us a chance to fine-tune our thinking and learn from the criticisms and ideas of many other thoughtful participants.

Finally, we would like to thank our publisher. The company has been through several mergers since we started this project, so we have enjoyed the opportunity to work with people who have been with us since the beginning and also with those who have become enthusiastic supporters of the game along the way. We've had valuable support from McGraw-Hill/Irwin people with responsibilities in editorial, design, production, marketing, sales, and technical support.

To all of these people—and to others who have encouraged us along the way—we are deeply grateful. Responsibility for any errors or omissions is certainly ours, but *The Marketing Game!* would not have been possible without the support of many others.

Table of Contents

1. Introduction to THE MARKETING GAME!

PLANNING MARKETING STRATEGY

Planning and implementing a marketing strategy is exciting—and challenging. To develop effective strategies, a marketing manager must analyze available market opportunities, understand and select target markets, and develop a marketing mix that will offer target customers superior customer value and give the firm an advantage over competitors. Many decisions are involved, and each decision relates to all of the others. Even a strategy that has proved to be very effective may need to change over time as customers' needs and competitors' strategies evolve. The fact that there is never a single best answer adds to the challenge—and to the opportunities.

Competition Makes a Difference

Competition is part of what makes marketing exciting—and an important part of why it's dynamic. Financial managers for different firms can use the same formula for figuring the return on an investment or the discounted present value of the investment. Accountants for competing firms can use the same commonly accepted practices in setting up their accounting records. Managers for competing companies also often use the same approaches for motivating employees. But, if marketing managers for competing firms just use the same strategy, the competition only becomes more intense. What will work—and work well—for an individual firm depends on the whole market—what needs customers have as well as how other competing firms are trying to meet those needs. But over time consumer expectations and needs may change, and competitors' strategies may change even more quickly.

Traditional approaches to learning about marketing strategy planning—reading about it in texts and articles, analyzing case situations, and working problems and exercises—can be very effective. These approaches provide useful frameworks and tools to help analyze the market and make good marketing decisions. But it is difficult for these approaches to give you a complete opportunity to put it all together—to put you in the driver's seat. The best way to have that kind of learning experience comes from making decisions, seeing the results of your decisions, and then refining the decisions over time.

Putting It All Together

That's where *The Marketing Game!* comes in—with a solution. It gives you an opportunity to learn by doing. You are a marketing manager for your firm. You analyze customers and their needs. You plan strategies—selecting target markets and blending product, place, promotion and price (the 4Ps) to develop a competitive advantage in the market. Of course, identifying a marketing mix that offers customers superior value also requires an understanding of competitors and their strengths and weaknesses.

In other words, you experience the excitement of being deeply involved in turning a market opportunity into results for your firm. And feedback about your results, competitors and customers gives you the opportunity to constantly improve your strategy. In sum, the game provides you with hands-on experiences that bring marketing concepts and ideas alive. It's fun. It's also challenging.

You might be wondering how all of these good things can be accomplished. It's a good question. And there's a straightforward answer. You make it happen. You bring it to life.

The pages that follow set the stage—and provide the background you need to bring the marketing management job to life. When you—and the managers for other firms—make decisions, a computer program (called TMGSim) analyzes all of the decisions and provides you with detailed feedback about what would have happened in a real marketplace. You don't need to know about the details of the computer program. In fact, after these first few pages you won't hear much about the role of the computer simulation on which *The Marketing Game!* competition is based. Rather, you will focus on understanding the market—and on making important decisions for your firm.

Reading the Text

You will quickly find that this book is not like other texts. In fact, it is more like an extended case study. The chapters are written as if they were a set of internal company reports and memos. These reports are not directed to you in your role as a student—they are directed to you in your role as marketing manager for the firm. The reports provide information about the market, the company, and your responsibilities—information you need to do your marketing management job.

Enough on that. Now, let's get on with the responsibilities of your new job.

WHAT'S AHEAD

You Are the New Marketing Manager

From now on, you can think of yourself as a new manager who has just joined the firm. At present, the firm develops and markets a handheld electronic device that controls computers via spoken commands. The previous marketing manager helped get the firm started, but he has now retired and the company wants you to take charge of its marketing effort—and help guide it in the decade ahead.

The President of the Firm Is Your Boss

Your instructor is the president of your firm. Like other top managers, you are responsible to the president of your firm. You will provide the president with your recommendations and decisions (your marketing plan)—and the president will help coordinate things with other departments as needed. For example, the president will make certain that the accounting department provides you with the financial summaries you need—and that you have a reasonable budget taking into consideration both your contributions to the profitability of the firm and what it takes to be effective in the market. The president will work with the production people to make certain that they produce the product you want for your target market and that it is available on schedule.

The president may direct you to collaborate with a team of managers to develop the firm's marketing plans, or alternatively you may be charged with sole responsibility for independently developing plans. The president may even expand your responsibilities—giving you authority to make decisions that are now based on company policy. For example, the president may give you the authority to design and introduce a totally new product, take over planning of sales promotion that is currently handled by an outside firm specializing in this area, or alter the way in which sales reps are paid.

To help you get off to a fast start in your new job, the president has given you this book—so you have the specific information you need to make good decisions. Before moving on to the specifics, however, it might be helpful for you to get an overview of what you will find in the upcoming chapters.

Chapter 2—The Market Opportunity

The president hired you to help bring a marketing orientation to the firm. Because you do not have previous experience with this firm—or its product, customers and competitors—the president has hired a consulting firm to prepare a report for your review. The president told the consultants that the report should provide an objective outside view of the market and company—to help you get up to speed faster.

Chapter 2 is the report prepared by the consulting firm. It describes the broad product-market in which the firm competes. It also discusses how firms in the market have operated in the past—and why. Directly and indirectly it also outlines some of the challenges and opportunities that need to be considered in developing effective marketing mixes and selecting a target market. You should read this report carefully because it provides much information that will help you make better decisions.

At the time of this writing, generally available information technology devices and software have not evolved to the extent that is portrayed in Chapter 2; yet, the product-market described is consistent with a direction that information technology is taking. Thus, the product-market situation is realistic and interesting. However, please keep in mind that you should *base your decisions on the information in this book and on the reports you receive as this market evolves over time, not on your guesses about how some computer hardware or software company may have handled a similar challenge in the past.* Remember, you are new to this company, its customers, and its competitors. The information you obtain along the way during the competition is the information on which you should base your plans.

Chapter 3—Marketing Department Responsibilities

You were hired because the previous marketing manager retired. When he announced his intention to retire, the president asked him to prepare a transition report—so that the new person who took over as marketing manager would know more about the marketing department's areas of responsibility.

Chapter 3 is the memo prepared by the previous marketing manager. It reviews company policies that affect the marketing department and explains some of the details of what needs to be considered in developing a marketing plan for the firm. It also discusses different marketing research reports and studies that are available to help you better understand your customers and competitors, and how you are doing in the market.

Chapter 4—Submitting the Annual Marketing Plan

As marketing manager, you need to develop marketing strategy and marketing plans for the future. Of course, these may need to be revised and updated each year to take into consideration feedback about how well the strategy is working, what competitors are doing, and other changes in the market.

At the beginning of each year, you will submit your marketing plan. The president has asked that the key decisions in your plan be summarized on a Marketing Plan Decisions Form. The form will make it easy for the president to review your plan because it summarizes the key decisions you'll make in each of your areas of responsibility. The president will tell you whether the Marketing Plan Decisions Form is to be submitted on paper, in digital form (as a computer file that you prepare with the TMGPlan software, discussed below), or both.

A staff assistant in the president's office has prepared a set of notes that explain the Marketing Plan Decisions Form. The assistant has also prepared samples of the various company reports and marketing research reports that are available to you.

Chapter 4 is the report prepared by the president's assistant. It includes important information about the firm's current financial situation and a summary of the results produced by the previous year's marketing plan. It also explains the budget constraints you face when preparing your initial marketing plan. So, it is the starting point on which you will build your decisions.

Chapter 5—Submitting an Expanded Marketing Plan

The president has been considering several changes in company policy—and these changes could have a direct effect on the marketing department and your responsibilities as marketing manager.

The president asked one of his assistants to prepare a brief memo that outlines the changes he has in mind. At the early point when the draft memo was prepared, the president had not made a final decision about the changes being considered. However, the president wanted to have the ideas in writing so that everyone could move quickly once the final decision was made.

Chapter 5 is the memo prepared by the president's assistant. The president may instruct you to read Chapter 4 and follow the guidelines established there—or instead to rely on the expanded guidelines presented in Chapter 5. In either event, the materials are ready and waiting for the president's decision.

Chapter 6—Supporting the Marketing Plan

The Marketing Plan Decisions Form that you will submit to the president each year provides a concise summary of the key decisions in your marketing plan. The president may also ask for other supporting information about the strategy on which the plan is based and what results you expect the plan to achieve.

A member of the president's staff has prepared several forms that will help you submit such supporting information. Chapter 6 is the material that the president's assistant has put together for you. It includes copies of a Marketing Budget Planning Form and a Marketing Strategy Summary Form—along with brief ideas on how each might be used.

The president may or may not ask you to complete these forms and submit a copy with your marketing plan. Either way, completing the forms can help you develop a better marketing plan—and make more effective use of your budget. And the completed forms will help you keep an organized record of your decisions and thinking over time.

Chapter 7—A New Market Opportunity

Chapter 7 is a second report prepared by the same outside consulting firm that prepared Chapter 2. At the end of that first report, the consultants mentioned that there might be a good opportunity for the firm to develop a completely new product. After reading the first report, the president asked the consultants to elaborate on their ideas in a report that detailed the pros and cons of the firm expanding its product line to include a new offering. The consultants have uncovered some interesting information. But at the same time, they conclude that the final decision about introducing a new product rests with the president— since any move in that direction will require additional resources and will lead the firm in new directions. The president has not yet decided if the firm should introduce the new product. The president may ask for your recommendations in that area—or even give you the authority to handle the new product decision yourself.

Appendix A—Marketing Plan Software

Finally, Appendix A was prepared by your firm's information technology staff. At the request of the previous marketing manager, the IT specialists have developed a microcomputer program that makes it faster to create and submit a password-protected electronic version of the Marketing Plan Decisions Form— and it also makes it easy to do some of the financial calculations and projections that are useful in marketing planning. Integrated with the firm's IT security, it allows managers who have an authorized password to get access to confidential company reports. The appendix provides instructions on using the computer program. However, these instructions are also available in an "online" help system and the program follows standard Windows approaches to make it easy to use.

CONCLUSION

The reports that are provided in the following chapters will give you a lot of useful information about your new job. The challenge is to analyze the opportunities and—within the constraints of your firm's resources—to develop a profitable marketing mix. As with most new jobs, it isn't expected that you will know everything you would like to know at the very beginning. Rather, there are some things you will learn at the start by studying the reports in this book and by applying your knowledge of marketing concepts; there are other things that you will learn during the competition based on experience, your evaluation of the feedback reports you get, the actions of competitors, and the like.

The president may elect to evaluate your performance on a variety of factors, but a primary objective of the firm is to increase its profitability over time. So, contribution to profit over time is certainly an important element of your evaluation. Good decisions will lead to effective strategies and that will earn profits, so earning profit is a sensible priority in *The Marketing Game!*

You will find many useful hints as you study the reports, and you will get other insights as you get feedback on the results of your plan decisions. So, we won't give you much other advice here. But, one general piece of advice is important. Specifically, just as is the case in the business world, you should know that there is not some "trick" or single "correct answer" in planning strategies for the game. There are a number of ways to succeed. And the best marketing plan depends on what target market you go after and on what competitors are doing. Finally, as in the real world, success by one firm doesn't doom a competing firm to failure. To the contrary, there are many opportunities for success in *The Marketing Game!*

We hope you will enjoy your new responsibilities. You face some interesting opportunities and challenges. We are confident that you will do the job well.

2. The Market Opportunity

Note: The president of your firm asked Market-Views, Inc.— a consulting firm— to prepare a report that would give you a concise but objective view of your company and the market in which it competes. This chapter is Market-Views' report.

INTRODUCTION

Your firm currently develops and markets a new type of voice recognition device (VRD) that has advanced capabilities for controlling computer applications based on "natural language" spoken commands. But the purpose of this report is not just to focus on what the company now produces—or how it currently operates. Rather, the objective is to provide you with a broader view of the market in which your firm competes. Understanding the market, your competitors, and other trends in the external environment will help you do a better job of identifying possible market opportunities. A good place to start is with some background information. It will help to put the current situation in perspective.

BACKGROUND

Technological Change

The development of practical electronic computers in the 1950s marked the beginning of fundamental changes in the U.S. technological base. At first, the changes were slow—because computers were very expensive and very hard to use. For the computer to be useful, potential customers needed faster and easier ways to tell the computer what to do. Computer companies realized that just making computers was not enough. They had to rethink their customers' needs—and how their products met customers' needs. Computer experts turned their attention to developing good software—computer programs that could be used to solve problems. As better software was developed, the use of mainframe computers spread much more rapidly—especially among businesses.

In the early stages, computer programmers who had special technical training were the only ones who used computers. They sent most instructions to the computer with keypunch cards. Each card consisted of 80 columns and each column on the card had a number of rows. Keypunch machines punched holes in each column of the card to designate a particular letter or number, and it often took a very large number of cards to send even a simple set of instructions to the computer. Thus, computer users often needed to prepare instructions on a large number of cards and then use an automated card reader machine to submit them to the computer all at once in a "batch."

This sort of batch process was time consuming and difficult because if there was a minor error in any instruction nothing would work—and creating error-free instructions required both patience and deep technical skill because the programming languages were complex. In addition, the process of punching holes in the keypunch cards, handling them, and processing them was plagued by mechanical errors.[1] Because of such problems, a computer user often had to read in a set of keypunch cards, wait for a printed report of errors from the computer, fix the errors one card at a time, and continue this process until the "job" finally ran correctly.

Over time this process became easier because the computer user could enter the commands at a computer terminal and store them on magnetic tape. With input from a terminal, the user could see many commands all at once, and updating programming instructions was faster, easier, and more reliable.

The pace of innovation picked up in the 1970s. Scientists invented new microchips that made it possible to produce powerful and economical desktop computers. Companies like Altair, Apple Computer, and Tandy Corporation (Radio Shack) saw the opportunity and entered the market with inexpensive microcomputers that were useful for both homes and businesses. Users of these early personal computers entered commands with a keyboard and the results appeared on the computer monitor. Entering information was often easier because it was an interactive process. A computer program that was stored on a floppy disk or cassette tape would prompt the user to answer a series of questions, and then after all of the questions were answered the program would run. This interactive approach significantly reduced the time-consuming error-correcting process that had been typical on "batch"-oriented mainframe computers.

Derived Demand for Microcomputer Software

As the power of microcomputers increased and the cost of the hardware dropped, demand grew rapidly. But software to communicate with and control the hardware continued to be a limitation. There was not much software

---

[1] Mechanical problems of this sort were a major source of controversy in the presidential election in 2000. Some voting places in Florida (and elsewhere) still relied on old-fashioned computer punch cards to record votes; when a card was not punched correctly, a hole was not created in the card but instead there might just be a "dimple" (impression in the card) or perhaps a "hanging chad" (partially punched hole). In such cases the cards/votes could not be processed by card reader machines, and manual inspection of the punch cards often led to inconsistent conclusions about the intent of the voter.

available for microcomputers. This started to change as growing demand attracted many firms to the market.

At first, the software firms were quite production oriented. A company could quickly develop a program and find many eager customers—even if the software did not meet their needs exactly. It seemed that any software was better than none.

A big breakthrough in software came when IBM introduced its personal computer. The IBM hardware was not that innovative. But there was a difference. Customers knew the IBM brand—and IBM made certain that software would be available. IBM developed some software itself. More important, however, IBM encouraged firms like Microsoft and Digital Research to develop software that would work on its computers. In addition, Compaq and other producers of PCs who entered the market designed their computers to be IBM-compatible. This meant that there were more potential customers for a given type of software since it would work on different machines. Furthermore, because other hardware standards were in place, there was an opportunity for independent firms to develop and market improved hardware "add on" equipment—like disk drives, graphics adapters, and printers.

Market Growth and Competition

Competition among both hardware and software firms increased as the market grew. With more products available and few barriers to entry, effective market segmentation was often the best way to achieve a competitive advantage. Software companies could avoid head-on competition by focusing on the needs of specific target markets—and developing marketing mixes to meet the needs of those customers.

Further, although the rate of growth in the general market for desktop personal computers started to slow down, new generations of technology in both hardware and software made it possible to add new hardware and software benefits specific to the needs of various market segments—and spark renewed sales. In some cases, the really innovative advances opened up new markets and resulted in new product life cycles.

For example, in the late 1980s and early 1990s advances in computer memory, processing speed, and disk storage made it possible to make computing easier— with operating systems, like IBM's OS/2 and Microsoft's Windows. These operating systems took advantage of the graphical user interface (GUI) idea that was originally developed, years earlier, by R&D efforts at Xerox's Palo Alto Research Center. The GUI made it much easier for a user to control computer software. The user no longer needed to memorize a host of specialized commands or be able to type them (without making errors) on a keyboard. Rather, full-screen displays offered instructions and simple choices. All the user had to do was "point and click" with a mouse to select the desired choice.

During the same period, miniaturization of electronic parts provided the impetus for small portable computers, such as Toshiba's popular notebooks (which ultimately became "laptops" as they got smaller) and for products like Apple's personal digital assistant, the Newton.

The Apple Newton and the concept of a personal digital assistant created an enormous amount of interest and attention. Of course, one benefit of this early PDA was its compact, handheld size. But another set of potential benefits related to the idea that the user could use a stylus (that is, an electronic pen) rather than a keyboard to write out information and communicate with the hardware. Unfortunately, the Newton didn't really deliver on all that it promised, and the PDA market didn't take off. On the other hand, a few years later another firm did a better job of implementing the same basic idea at a lower price with its Palm Pilot. Executives who traveled a lot were among the first to adopt it, but its popularity quickly spread to other segments.

In the same way that these innovations opened new markets, other firms—like Novell and Microsoft—were experiencing real growth in demand for the hardware and software solutions they had developed to help people who work in groups to share information among networks of personal computers. By the early 1990s networks were a major force.

Similarly, the 1990s marked the introduction and explosive growth of multimedia computing—which blends full motion video, voice, pictures and other types of graphics, along with traditional text, numerical data, and computer control. The use of CD-Rom and DVD media, digital sound processors, scanners, and video cams provided versatile ways to get multimedia content into and out of the computer. The effects of these developments were far reaching. For example, producers of computers designed primarily for games were able to incorporate more realistic images, animation, and sound in their software. Similarly, some educational materials (like encyclopedias) that had in the past only been available in book form were able to incorporate video clips, interviews, and photos.

Late in the decade of the 1990s all of the innovations that had been occurring in the computing arena came together with the development and explosive growth of the Internet and the World Wide Web. The Web made it simple to connect computers and easy for a user to "surf" the Internet, usually by simply clicking a mouse on a "hyper linked" word or image. In turn, the standards that resulted from the growth of the Internet prompted an explosion of "in house" intranets within companies. Because the internet created a network that tied together almost all computers, it prompted explosive growth in the use of email, computer file exchanges (for example, transfer of MP3 music files via Napster-like websites), flash files with full-motion graphics, and server-based software applications (for example, where the user goes to a website and uses a software tool--like a home mortgage payments calculator--available at that site.).

All of these changes have resulted in a real revolution in computing and information technology—with customers enjoying new benefits on many fronts. In such a dynamic market it is difficult to know what potential opportunities will prove best for the future—but there definitely are opportunities and some of the most promising ones focus on even simpler ways to communicate with computers—using computer voice recognition technologies.

The idea of talking to a computer and having it do what is asked isn't new. It's been around for over 40 years. As an ideal, it is obviously superior to some combination of sitting at a keyboard, clicking a mouse, or using a hand-writing stylus; it makes computer punch cards seem all the more ancient as a way of controlling computers. But the ideal has been hard to achieve. Until recently most personal computers didn't have the power to handle voice recognition. Even after the new generation of multimedia PCs came on the scene, firms had only limited success in creating and selling software-based voice recognition systems. The processors were not developed to do that work, and it was difficult to "train" voice recognition software to respond to individual differences in speech. Even in the best cases error rates in translating what was said to digital form were usually too high.

In spite of these problems, marketing research indicates that customers are really interested in the potential benefits of computer voice recognition. Many say that they would be willing to buy a voice recognition product, even if it was not from a well-known company, if it really offered a breakthrough and made voice recognition work well. For example, the research indicates that they want to be able to control a computer with "natural language" voice commands rather than by typing complex messages on the keyboard or by clicking a mouse. They also want to be able to create the electronic content for word processing, email, spreadsheet, and database applications by speaking rather than typing. They want a handheld device with a convenient wireless link to a standard computer. And of course they want the device to adjust to their individual accents and voice patterns with few errors.

Managers at a high tech start-up firm thought that they could meet the important needs identified by the research. So, they raised investment money to support the significant research and development effort needed to try to solve the problems. After several false starts, the technical folks came up with a real breakthrough—and the firm was able to obtain patents that gave it a virtual monopoly in producing a new type of microchip that was optimized for processing spoken language commands—that is, voice recognition.

The firm had the resources and the capabilities to produce the microchip it had designed--and to improve the quality of the invention over time. But, it also faced limitations. It did not have the expertise to create the "instruction set" software that the chip would use to convert spoken words into computer commands. Similarly, the firm didn't have the experience required to design the case and wireless controls that would integrate the microchip and software into a finished product. The founders of the firm even admitted that they didn't know how to figure out what specific combination of voice recognition features would really satisfy customers and at the same time be profitable.

Unless these challenges can be addressed, the technological breakthrough will be wasted. After all, customers are not interested in a microchip per se—but rather are interested in the benefits of a working voice recognition product.

Cooperation among Software and Hardware Producers

This reality prompted the firm to think about an alliance—a formal partnership with other firms that had different capabilities. That way, the microchip firm could license its technology to its partners, and then those firms could in turn take over in the value adding process to create a finished voice recognition device and market it.

This background can give you important insights into the forces that led to the growth of your own company.

A NEW OPPORTUNITY

Potentially, a large number of different firms might be candidates to make such an alliance succeed. But, the microchip firm felt that it was better to have a very close working relationship with a few firms rather than to be spread too thin working with whoever was willing to license the technology. A close relationship was also important because it was absolutely critical to have a high-quality device with the relevant software available quickly when the microchip or anticipated updated versions of it were first introduced. And—to take full advantage of the microchip's new capabilities—the software developers would need to know details of the microchip's design in advance.

So, the microchip producer turned to some firms that were small but skillful in the area of voice recognition software and the sort of device that would be required. It urged them to join in the effort of developing the product-market for voice recognition needs. Specifically, the computer firm agreed to provide the software developers with confidential information about the microchip design—and promised to tell them about changes in its proprietary hardware before it introduced new models. In return for this information, a "partner" company had to agree that it would focus full attention on developing the software and other aspects of the device that would be based on the microchip.

Four firms with relevant hardware and software experience entered into such agreements with the computer company. Although the four companies would be competing among themselves on equal terms, they alone would have the information (and technology license agreements) needed to develop certain types of voice recognition devices for this market. Other companies would be able to develop other specialized applications for the microchip—like voice-activated controls for equipment to assist people who faced the limits of physical paralysis. But, the primary voice recognition device for personal computers could only be developed by these four companies.

All of this planning and "partnering" paid off. Sales of the initial devices took off—even in the first year. Further, each of the four device makers created and introduced its own successful new product. Your firm and the other three firms continue to grow and prosper as interest in control of computers via voice recognition grows in popularity.

12

COMPETITORS IN A BROAD PRODUCT-MARKET

These four competitors are all focused on the same broad product-market. The broad product-market consists of businesses and final consumers in our country who have an interest in controlling computer applications with natural voice commands. While these firms are part of the overall personal computer or computer "accessories" industry—they also think of themselves as a separate industry since they alone compete in the product-market for this specialized, processor-based voice recognition device (VRD).

Each of the VRD firms has focused on developing a combined hardware/software device to translate "natural language" into digital commands because it is one area where the license agreement and special knowledge of the microchip's design limit further competition. In addition, almost everyone who wants to experience the benefits of easier control of their computer needs some sort of VRD.

Since your firm is so heavily involved in this area, let's take a closer look at what needs are met by voice recognition devices.

Benefits Offered by Hardware-Based Voice Recognition Devices

With the right computer support, a VRD offers many powerful capabilities that translate to benefits for users. At one level, the device allows the user to capture spoken words and convert them into computer commands to control specific software applications (for functions such as word processing, email, Internet browsing, spreadsheets, manipulating MP3 music files, etc.). It can also record spoken words (say, the content for an email message) and create an electronic text file without requiring the user to type. In that regard, the software provides the user with many of the capabilities of a digital "dictation" system—but at low cost. For example, an executive might use the device to prepare the script for a speech or a computer-aided presentation. A home user might use the dictation features to prepare a letter or email message to relatives.

Such a device also allows the user to "cut and paste" audio voice recordings and electronic text files and merge them together. The right device makes it easy to experiment with different effects and approaches, and then "undo" any step that doesn't work as intended. New material may be added or deleted easily.

There are, however, some disadvantages to VRD. Some people still have trouble learning about the basic operation of a VRD. For example, the device must be "trained" to recognize special voice commands from each user. Further, for many people, using vocal commands is a really new idea and requires them to think in new ways. Thus, learning how to use specific VRD capabilities takes time—and may require special training. Even an experienced user can encounter problems. For example, it's possible for a device's natural language "translators" to accidentally convert a spoken command in the wrong way, and when that happens the computer application can wipe out a carefully prepared file (say for a multimedia presentation) before it has been saved for later use. Further, the combined cost of a powerful computer, software applications, and the VRD is high.

Some customers compare these front-end costs (the investment in training and equipment) to the time and costs they can save later. For example, a company may be able to develop reports or presentations that can then be used by many different salespeople in the field—so they can save time preparing sales presentations and still do a better job during sales calls. Other customers are not trying to save money—they just want to learn something new and have some fun.

Many users of the new VRD think that the benefits far outweigh the limitations. In fact, many people use their VRDs and computers primarily for one type or another of computer application. As a result, demand for VRDs is strong—and growth in the market is expected as more people learn about what VRDs can do.

Product-Market Segments

In the beginning, no one was certain who would buy a VRD. So each VRD firm focused on designing a good general-purpose device that would take advantage of the microchip's most significant capabilities. After all, customers bought a VRD primarily to get a faster and easier way to control their computers. Each VRD firm tried to develop one marketing mix that would do a pretty good job of meeting the needs of different market segments. This approach seemed to make sense in the beginning. It resulted in target markets that were large enough to be profitable. Now, however, problems are surfacing. All four firms offer VRDs and have developed marketing mixes that are very similar. Although the number of potential customers has increased, competition is intense. There is a good opportunity to find profitable submarkets.

VRDs produced by the four firms are purchased both by final consumers and by businesses. The variety of final users ranges from sophisticated power users to grade-school students. While some of these potential customers are using faster or more powerful computer equipment, the basic capabilities are the same. Conversely, it is also clear that some of their VRD needs are very different since potential customers focus on different applications/functions (i.e., benefits) within the broad set of capabilities.

Market-Views' research reveals that most potential customers in the broad product-market can be classified into more homogeneous market segments. Market-Views has identified six main segments. Each segment has a nickname—to make it easier to remember. A description of each segment is provided below.

▶ The Modern Students

The modern students are college students who use a VRD to work on term projects, other school-related assignments, and to pursue their extracurricular interests, including communications with family and friends. This is encouraged by colleges that want to be seen as innovators in educational technology. They have made VRD technology a priority—in some cases even installing VRD wireless "receivers" on "networked" computers in computer labs, dorms, and classrooms so that a student can easily use his or her own VRD on the available computers. Many of the modern students can't afford to buy a powerful computer of their own—but they can use one of the many available on campus. Even with access to a free computer, they want an economical VRD of their own to access and control the information technology resource materials available to them. Economy is a major concern for this budget-constrained segment.

Students in this segment often form user groups or informally share advice to help each other get the full benefits of a VRD—or to solve VRD problems. Many campuses also have computer support centers that answer questions about hardware and software, including VRD applications. With so much help available, students don't seem to be particularly worried about learning to use a VRD or about problems they might encounter. As one student put it, "help from my roommate is better than any tutorial." Modern students accounted for about 20 percent of VRD sales last year. The VRD is proving to be very popular on campuses—and this submarket will probably continue to grow for some time.

▶ The Home Users

The home users segment contains a mix of households who use a simple VRD to do a variety of computing work—everything from surfing the Internet "from an armchair" to creating recipe files to preparing entries in a daily diary. In some homes, people even use a VRD to leave each other messages. For example, rather than just leave a list of things that need to be done, they quickly dictate an "enhanced" message with all the relevant details and print it or even email it to another member of the family. Different members of the household may use the VRD for different reasons—but typically what they are doing is not very complicated given available technology. They're just having fun.

The home users are pretty much on their own--so they prefer software that is easier to learn. They seem only moderately concerned about error protection, perhaps because their uses of a VRD are not for critical job-related matters; on the other hand, they may become more sensitive about error protection over time if they make errors that waste a lot of time. Money for a VRD usually must come from some other area of the household budget—so most home users have only limited interest in high-priced VRDs. Last year, the home users segment accounted for about 15 percent of total sales.

▶ The Harried Assistants

The harried assistants segment consists of secretaries, administrative assistants, and other employees who spend at least some of their time preparing and revising materials for other people in their firms. For example, the boss may sketch out the ideas for what is to go in a sales proposal, then the assistant is expected to use the VRD to quickly pull everything together into a polished presentation; or, an administrative assistant may need to update department expense reports for the accounting people. Without special VRD support, doing these jobs could be a massive headache and take a long time, but with a good VRD it's just becoming a normal part of the assistant's job. In fact, some companies have found that the same amount of work can be done by fewer assistants once they become skilled with a VRD.

However, turnover in these jobs is high and often the assistants are just learning about a VRD—making the switch from preparing materials the old-fashioned way. Thus, they want software that is not too hard to learn or use. Very quickly they must be able to use a VRD to prepare many routine assignments. Moreover, one assistant often needs to satisfy requests from a number of different bosses—so the harried assistants need a VRD that can handle a variety of needs. Most assistants worry about having difficulties with a VRD. They seem to have good reason to worry; bosses who themselves don't work with a VRD (or for that matter, even a computer!) are not very understanding when there is a problem.

Although the assistants may influence the choice of a particular VRD—others in the company usually make the final purchase decision. In addition, companies often purchase a number of VRDs at the same time—so that different assistants will be using the same device. Last year, sales to this segment amounted to approximately 25 percent of total sales.

▶ *The Professional Creators*

The professional creators segment consists of people who have professions in which they rely heavily on computers to create varied types of content materials—their "deliverable" output. For example, this group includes journalists and other types of writers, financial analysts who create spreadsheets and databases, advertising agency people who create ad copy and images, package designers, and many others who create and modify some sort of "documents" for a living. Of all the segments, this group spends the most time using a computer and therefore the most time working with a VRD. Professional creators are often the innovators—among the first to use VRD capabilities. For example, a graphics designer might use a VRD in combination with relevant software applications to help translate visual concepts into actual layouts and images "on the fly." This work might include voice recognition created notes and annotation about what he is trying to accomplish. He would worry about final "polishing" later after he has initial feedback from a client. As this suggests, the professional creators are primarily concerned with speed and special commands for advanced capabilities. The right VRD helps them to be more creative more quickly—and by saving them time and producing a better product they can improve their earnings. Sales to this segment accounted for about 10 percent of last year's total sales.

▶ *The High-Tech Managers*

High-tech managers buy a VRD primarily for their own use on the job. Usage tends to be higher when they are "on the road" (working with a laptop); at the office they often rely on a secretary or other assistant to do routine computer work. The managers use a VRD less than most users--but when traveling (and sometimes at the office), they use a VRD to make it easier and faster to do some special types of work themselves. For example, they might use a VRD during the evening in a hotel room to "whip out" a report that includes a complex spreadsheet—with fancy graphics—to highlight the results of a financial analysis.

Members of this segment are very interested in the number of capabilities offered. They take pride in the status of knowing about and using the very latest developments—and they don't want their colleagues to think they are just doing plain old "dictation" work that a secretary could do. Thus, their choices when purchasing a VRD are partially motivated by social needs for status and esteem. Some in this segment buy a VRD and learn to use it just because it's "in," not because it will make that much difference in their productivity.

The high-tech managers pick the brand of VRD they want—but the company pays for it. Last year, sales to this segment accounted for nearly 22 percent of the total.

▶ *The Concerned Parents*

The concerned parents are generally two-career professional couples with school-age children. These affluent—but busy—couples want to provide their kids with all of the advantages of high-tech learning—and that includes making computing faster and easier. They see VRD as an important trend for the future and want to get their kids interested in and experienced with it early. They also see a VRD as providing a valuable educational experience. They want a simple VRD that children can learn and use themselves. Last year, the concerned parents accounted for 8 percent of total unit sales.

MARKET POTENTIAL

The Market Is Growing

The broad product-market appears to be in the early middle part of the growth stage of the product life cycle. Industry experts think that growth in industry sales will continue for a number of years—perhaps for as much as a decade. Many experts believe that there is ample growth to fuel better profits for the whole industry—and for individual firms. However, even the optimists are unwilling to make precise forecasts too far into the future.

There is agreement, however, that the growth in market potential—what a whole segment might buy—will depend on several factors. These include the size of the segment, growth trends, the extent to which potential customers are aware of VRDs and what they can do, and how well the marketing mix (including customer service after the sale) meets customers' needs.

Some Segments Are Growing Faster than Others

At present, the size of the various market segments differs substantially. Research found the harried assistants to be the largest segment with 25 percent of total unit sales last year. The concerned parents segment was the smallest with 8 percent. Current sales may provide a snapshot of the opportunity offered by each segment. However, sales to the different segments have grown at different rates. This can be seen in Exhibit 2A—which shows estimates of unit sales to each segment during the past three years.

Exhibit 2A: Estimates of Unit Sales to Each Segment during Past 3 Years

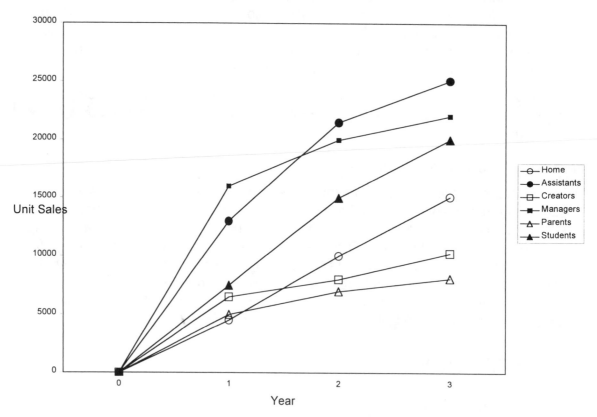

Of course, simply extending these trends could be dangerous—since factors behind the trends may change. In addition, these sales figures are estimates based on a marketing research survey of VRD users. Some people who responded to the survey couldn't recall exactly when they purchased the device—so it is best not to view these figures as exact.

Interpret Exhibit 2A with some caution. The large or fast-growing segments—in terms of unit sales—may not be the best targets. Some segments may prove to be more profitable than others—depending on how much it costs to develop a marketing mix that will meet their needs and depending on the price they will pay. It may also be possible to develop a marketing mix that targets more than one segment in a combined target market.

Advertising May Make More Customers Aware

Industry experts agree that the overall level and nature of industry advertising will affect market growth. Many customers still are unfamiliar with voice recognition devices and what they do. Higher overall spending on advertising will help to inform more potential customers—and more of them are likely to enter the market. Because the life cycle is still in its growth stage, advertising so far has focused on building awareness and informing consumers about the product

Mason & Perreault

class. Advertising that helps pioneer the market may help your own firm—but it may also help competitors. On the other hand, competitive advertising focused on specific brands may increase a firm's share of the market now and in the future—even if it does less to stimulate overall market growth.

Marketing Mix Must Meet Customers' Needs

It is important to emphasize that growth in the broad product-market—or in segments of the market—will depend on how successfully available marketing mixes meet customers' needs. At present, some customers are buying a VRD that is not exactly what they want—they just purchase whatever is available that comes closest to their ideal.

On the other hand, many potential customers just wait. They will not buy anything until just the right product is available in the right place at the right price. Further, different segments have different needs. Thus, different marketing strategies—different marketing mixes for different target markets—may be required.

This last point is an important one—since the four firms in the market are at present all offering pretty much the same marketing mix.

TYPICAL MARKETING MIXES

Product

There can be many technical differences in VRDs, especially in how the "instruction set" software works. But research shows that most customers tend to simplify their evaluation process by grouping VRD features into three main areas: (1) the number and variety of special commands, (2) protection against user errors, and (3) ease of learning.

▶ *Special Commands*

All VRDs offer many of the same basic commands. Standard commands allow the user to convert vocal dictation into electronic text or audio files, to edit the files they have created, and to use voice to control the standard functions (like opening or saving a file) common to most software applications. In addition to such standard commands, a VRD may have a variety of more advanced command "sets." These command sets, generally referred to as "special commands" tend to be specific to the varied types of software required for specific applications—ranging from database or spreadsheet applications to graphics programs to Internet browsers and video games. Examples of these include commands to control navigation of Internet browsers, to add special effects to full motion video, to cut out backgrounds from digital pictures, and to control the actions of figures in animated video games.

Not all VRD customers want a lot of special commands. It doesn't help to have a VRD with a command set that the customer doesn't want or need. Further, having more special commands can also lead to errors—since it makes it more difficult for the VRD to "parse" natural language statements and determine the specific intent of the user. For example, saying a command by accident, using it in the wrong way, or in the wrong software application may produce undesirable results that are hard to change. Even so, users in certain target markets seem to have an appetite for special commands that allow them to have voice control over more different aspects of their computing work.

▶ Error Protection

Some VRDs are designed to prevent users from accidentally doing something wrong. At first this may sound good—but there is a trade-off. A VRD with more error protection is usually slower to use. A simple example will make this more concrete. A natural language statement made by a user might be interpreted by a VRD as meaning that a paragraph of text or a picture should be deleted. This would be a common command in revising a VRD-created "document" or in many other types of applications. But, much work could be lost unintentionally if a user issues the delete command by accident or if the VRD interpreted some other command incorrectly. Thus, some users like a "conservative" VRD that protects them with an "are you sure" warning on the VRD's LCD panel when it thinks they have issued a delete command. But that warning slows things down. On the other hand, expert users are more precise and just want the VRD to execute the command. All programs have some level of error protection. But, the extent of such error protection can vary substantially—and in total it affects how quick and convenient it is to use a VRD. In short, some people like a lot of error protection. Others think that defeats part of the benefit of a VRD and they prefer to do things faster.

▶ Ease of Learning

Another feature concerns how easy it is to learn to use a VRD and to train it to the user's unique speech patterns. Some customers are worried about how long it will take to get going—and how much help is available if there is a problem. Different aspects of the VRD maker's product may address this concern. The device itself can be created to partially automate the "training" process so that it gets better at interpreting vocal commands as the user corrects mistakes. But, there are other approaches. VRD companies can provide videotape or Web-based tutorials along with the device—so the user can see how everything works. Others offer built-in VDR-based interactive training capabilities that lead a novice through each step of "training" the device to recognize individual voice patterns.

Not everyone is interested in all of this. In fact, some may see it as a problem. A VRD that is designed to be easy to "train" may be less reliable if the VRD is later used in varying sound environments—say when there is background noise from a TV or air conditioning unit. Similarly, detailed tutorials are often paced too slowly and explain things the knowledgeable customer already knows, or make it take longer to find an answer. It is also true that a VRD that is easy to learn (early on) may also be more cumbersome to use (later on). For example, other things equal it is easier to learn how to use a VRD that has fewer capabilities.

But later, when the user knows all of the basics, it might be better to have more capabilities (even if they were a bit more fuss to learn in the first place).

▶ *Product Modifications*

Changes in technology as well as feedback and suggestions from customers mean that firms are continually doing research and development and updating and modifying their VRD products. In fact, all four firms in this market now have a yearly revision cycle that corresponds to updates in the underlying microchip. The start of each fiscal year brings announcements of new versions and models of VRDs in time for the dealer trade shows. In some instances, there may be major changes in the product features as firms attempt to better meet the needs of their target customers. In other cases only minor modifications are made to accommodate changes and additions to the microchip or to the computer hardware and software that the VRD controls. In general, large changes in a single year tend to significantly stress the R&D department and require use of expensive overtime or contract programmers.

As part of the license agreement with the producer of the microchip, all four of the VRD firms must stick to some standards for the way a VRD "interprets" spoken language and converts it to computer commands. Thus, a person who has become familiar with one firm's VRD can usually switch to a new VRD from a competing company with very little hassle or "switching cost." Having a "standard" for the command structure has helped the voice recognition industry grow, but there is also a potential downside. Specifically, consumers who are considering upgrading to a new model VRD product may not be hesitant to switch to a competing brand—if it does a better job of meeting their needs. In other words, each firm in this market must constantly "earn" the loyalty of its customers.

Place

▶ *Indirect Distribution*

All four firms sell their VRDs through middlemen who in turn sell direct to final customers. Some of the middlemen focus on sales to business customers, and some of them focus on sales to final consumers. Thus, in a technical sense, some of them are wholesalers and some of them are retailers. Regardless of their primary customer focus, they all refer to themselves as dealers.

When VRDs were first introduced, several firms attempted to sell VRDs directly from their own websites as well as through dealers. This approach didn't generate many sales because most potential customers for VRDs in this early stage simply didn't believe that the devices would deliver the benefits claimed. Some skepticism was justified; earlier software-based voice recognition systems did not perform very well. In any event, most customers wanted to see a live demonstration of the product and have the opportunity to ask a salesperson specific questions. The full-service dealers who had convenient locations, stock on hand, and knowledgeable sales reps met this need. However, as one irate dealer put it, "I'm not happy about having to compete with my own supplier for sales, especially given what I'm investing to create customers." Because of sentiments like this, many dealers dropped brands of VRDs that were being sold direct in favor of ones that were not. Rather than lose distribution, VRD firms that were selling from their own websites promised to replace the "buy now" button on their websites with a dealer-locator feature. That was some time ago, but it's hard for them to go back on that promise now.

▶ Dual Distribution

Although firms that produce VRDs no longer sell direct to final customers, all four firms do currently rely on dual channels of distribution to reach the market. The two channels involve different types of dealers, and the different dealers tend to attract different types of customers.

▶ Full-Service Dealers (Channel 1)

The dealers in one channel typically serve local customers with a carefully chosen line of computers, computer software, and computer accessories that they carry in stock. Some of these dealers are "independents" and some are part of a larger chain. Although many of them have some sort of website, they tend to focus on in-store sales. The good ones have well-trained salespeople who provide customers with technical information, demonstrations, and personalized service before and after the sale.

These dealers are especially attractive to customers who want to be able to see and compare different products—and to customers who want the assurance of having the supplier nearby in case of problems. In fact, the price these full-service dealers charge usually includes a service agreement that extends the typical 90-day warranty on a VRD device to a full year and offers "same day" replacement if a VRD has a problem. This is attractive "insurance" to a user who routinely relies on a VRD.

It was these full-service dealers who helped the VRD producers with the effort to pioneer the market and get early sales from skeptical customers. Thus, for convenience we will refer to them as Channel 1. In the early days these dealers were willing to handle the VRD because it was a new idea and it gave them a product that was distinctive relative to what was available from Internet or mail-order discounters. At that time, the discounters focused on products that were already popular, would turn over fast without much personal selling effort, and didn't require much customer "hand-holding."

▶ Discount Dealers (Channel 2)

However, as the market for VRDs grew, more Internet and mail-order discount dealers became interested in carrying the VRD products. The dealers in this channel (Channel 2) offer more limited service and handle larger assortments of products. They also offer lower prices and tend to have more rigid policies concerning product returns; it can be a hassle for a customer to get a return merchandise authorization (rma). If there is an after-sale quality problem, they usually don't have their own service facilities so there are often delays in getting repairs.

For the bulk of their business, these discounters rely on orders placed at an Internet website or by toll-free telephone call or fax. These dealers are mainly order takers—they don't provide much service or help to customers. They can't demonstrate products for customers, and because of the very wide assortments of products they carry their salespeople often don't know the details of any of them very well. Rather, they primarily appeal to price-sensitive customers as well as to customers who don't have a local supplier with the right selection.

▶ Distribution Intensity

At present, producers of VRDs are in general not attempting to obtain intensive distribution (i.e., making their products available through all suitable and available dealers) in either channel. Rather, it appears that your firm and competitors are trying to sell through about 30 percent of the available dealers in each channel.

When VRDs were first introduced, the best full-service dealers were not willing to carry a brand unless the producer provided exclusive distribution agreements within the dealer's main geographic markets—at least for a two year introductory period. Some other dealers didn't want to handle the devices at all because their customers had been unhappy with software voice recognition products--and they projected that sales volume would be low. Now that the market is growing, however, more dealers are interested in handling the product. Further, having a brand of VRD more widely available might increase sales and market share—in part because it is more convenient to more customers and in part because of it is being pushed by more dealers.

On the other hand, there's no "free lunch" when it comes to increasing distribution intensity. For one thing, some dealers don't do a very good job or contribute much to sales volume, and dealing with them may require more expense and hassle (for example, additional sales reps to call on them, deal with problems, etc.). Further, the best dealers are now already handling some brand(s) of VRD; getting them to add another brand of VRD (or switch from one they already carry) is tough.

Another issue concerns competition among dealers. Many customers still want help in deciding what VRD to buy (or if to buy at all). Yet, dealers won't put as much effort into a brand that is available from many other competing dealers. The larger the number of dealers with the same product just encourages more price competition, thinner margins, and lower profits.

Trade promotion is also an issue. Specifically, if firms in the industry start to make more aggressive use of trade promotion, dealers will expect it and use it as a bargaining lever. If that happens, more sales promotion spending will become a requirement to keep a larger number of dealers actively selling a particular brand of VRD.

In short, the dealers in the two channels provide different marketing functions and tend to appeal to different types of customers. The different types of dealers also require different kinds of promotional attention from the VRD producers.

Promotion

Promotion blends in the VRD business include sales promotion, personal selling, and advertising. In addition, firms try to get publicity in computer magazines and other trade publications, and they try to encourage good word-of-mouth endorsements among consumers. VRD producers target most of their advertising toward final customers, but their personal selling and sales (trade) promotion efforts are targeted at the dealers.

► *Personal Selling*

Personal selling is important to VRD producers. Each firm maintains its own staff of trained sales representatives. These salespeople sell to the dealers who in turn sell to the final customer. To better serve the needs of the different dealers, the sales force specializes by channel. Thus, any one salesperson works either with the traditional dealers or with Internet mail-order discount dealers—but not both.

Sales representatives do a mix of selling and supporting tasks. Selling tasks involve getting orders from current dealers as well as developing new accounts. Selling tasks also include persuading dealers to put more emphasis on pushing the firm's brand (for example, with better personal selling effort of their own). The supporting tasks include explaining technical details, training the dealers' sales staffs, and keeping the dealers up-to-date on new developments—including changes in sales promotion deals available from the firm.

The percent of personal selling effort spent on support activities tends to vary with the amount of service that the dealers provide to their customers. Dealers that provide a lot of service and selling help to their customers in turn look for more support and training from the VRD producer(s) whose product they sell.

► *Advertising*

VRD producers advertise in many media—trade and computer magazines, publications such as Business Week and Newsweek, and even on television and radio. Internet banner ads that link to company websites are also widely used. Each VRD producer has its own website, and these sites promote the specific advantages of the firm's brand of VRD, provide "dealer finder" wizards, and other useful information.

Last year advertising expenditures by the four producers totaled $1 million, or an average of $250,000 per firm. Firms use various types of advertising depending on their objectives. These types may be grouped into the five categories summarized below:

Pioneering advertising works to build primary demand—or demand for the whole product category—rather than promoting a specific brand. In the past, this was an important type of advertising since consumers needed to become aware of the possibilities of VRDs. Even now, there's a very substantial untapped market of consumers who do not know about VRDs, what they do, or why someone might benefit by using one.

Direct competitive advertising attempts to build selective demand (and share of market) for a firm's own brand. Its focus is on features of the current model and the main objective is immediate buying action, with relatively less carryover to future years.

Indirect competitive advertising also attempts to build selective demand, but it tends to focus on influencing future purchases—so that when a customer is ready to buy, he or she will choose that brand.

Reminder advertising reinforces earlier promotion and merely tries to keep the brand's name before the consumer. It doesn't do much good if customers are not already familiar with the brand, but it can be quite efficient if the brand is already well known and has a following of satisfied customers.

Corporate (institutional) advertising focuses on promoting the overall firm rather than a specific product. Because firms in this industry have a single product at this point, corporate advertising has not been used much. Corporate ads that have been run have not had clear objectives. However, if firms in the industry introduce other products, this may change. Corporate ads might then focus on positioning themes that are effective for promoting some primary product but also producing favorable spillover for a firm's other product(s). This might be a way to build interest across products at lower cost.

▶ *Sales Promotion*

Sales promotion is a relatively new tool for the VRD producers. In fact, so far each of the four VRD firms has turned to outside specialists to help plan sales promotions.

Dealers are the target of most of the sales promotion—which includes trade show presentations, special brochures, dealer sales contests, and a variety of "deals" to the trade. Deals seem to be quite popular. For example, a producer might offer a dealer additional products free with a purchase of a certain quantity.

The objective of these trade promotions is to encourage the dealer to carry and push a particular brand or to devote special attention to selling it. This has caused some concern among the VRD producers. Some think that sales promotion simply increases each firm's costs. They think that a firm that doesn't do sales promotion will lose market share—but that no one gains if everyone is offering basically the same types of promotion. In other words, promotions seem to impact a firm's market share—positively if it is the only firm running a promotion (or spends more on the promotion) or negatively if it is the only firm without a promotion. However, if everyone is offering trade promotions they may just increase costs without much real benefit to anyone, except the dealers.

Because the firms in this market have not been using sales promotion very long, it's too early to know if these concerns are valid. But sales promotion is often more effective in prompting short-term responses than in building longer-term brand insistence.

▶ Publicity and Word-of-Mouth

VRD firms in the industry have in general enjoyed favorable publicity—primarily coverage in computer magazines read by both dealers and final consumers. In general, the magazines provide reviews of updated models of the device, and tout the advantages of whatever is different. Thus, the general effect of publicity has been favorable for the industry.

However, a major consumer publication recently published ratings of the help that users of different brands of VRDs were able to get from customer service telephone lines and at support sections of websites. Unfortunately, the news was not all positive, and it hurt some firms' sales. The magazine gave low customer service ratings to several firms whose support did not keep pace with their growth in customers. This, coupled with negative word-of-mouth, resulted in shifts in market share to companies that were offering the best customer service. To counter this, companies that had earned weak customer service ratings increased their spending on customer service. Now there is once again not much difference among firms in after-the-sale customer service. But, that may change if some firms try to use service as a basis for competitive advantage.

Customer service must be carefully managed; at a minimum the recent ratings published by the magazine call attention to firms that don't provide adequate service. On a more positive note, superior customer service probably translates to some increase in market share. However, the cost of providing customer service—like other expenses—must be covered in the price a VRD firm charges.

Price

Suggested retail list prices for VRDs have ranged from $150 to $400 depending on the features of the device, the manufacturer, and the channel(s) in which it is distributed.

The VRD producer decides on a wholesale price at which to sell to the dealers. The dealers then decide what retail price to charge their customers. Thus, the producer can't actually control the price to the final customer. But this is not a significant problem. Dealers tend to stick to the same price-setting approaches. Thus, the producer can get a pretty good idea what the price will be at the end of the channel.

▶ Dealers Set the Retail Price

Dealers typically set the retail price by using a customary markup percent. The markup percent is different in the two channels. The difference is in part due to differences in the amount of service provided by the dealers (including the after-sale extended warranty) and differences in the quantities they sell. The customary markup by dealers in Channel 1 is 50 percent. Dealers in Channel 2 use a 35 percent markup. The formula for the markup percent is:

Dealer markup percent = (Retail selling price – Wholesale price) / (Retail selling price).

Note that these dealers figure markup percents that are based on the retail selling price.

While the middlemen in the two channels rely on standard markups to determine their selling price, pricing by the VRD producers must be based on consideration of their costs and on estimates of the demand curve. There are several reasons why producers can't use a standard markup percent. First, costs of producing the actual VRD devices and documentation are small compared to the costs of product development. Second, the most profitable quantity may not be what would sell at a price based on a standard markup percent.

The VRD producers do announce a suggested retail price. Dealers are not obligated to sell the software at that price, but it may be difficult for them to ask for more than that amount. However, they can quite easily charge a lower price. In fact, price cutting is common among the discount mail-order houses. This is reflected in their lower markup percent.

The discounters may cut the price even further if they have been offered a sales promotion deal of some sort by a producer. In effect, some of these deals lower the dealer's cost per product. In the discount channel, the dealers tend to pass along some of their savings to customers—in the form of a lower retail price. By contrast, most traditional dealers just view a deal from the producer as a way for them to make a higher profit per unit.

▶ *Customer Price Perceptions*

Consumer research suggests that most VRD customers have in mind a reference price—the retail price they expect to pay for a VRD. However, different VRD users tend to look at the retail price in different ways—and the reference price is not the same for everybody. Some people think that the price indicates the quality of the device—and for them a higher reference price is better; they interpret a low price as a signal of low quality. Others believe that the price has little to do with the actual quality. Instead, they think of quality in terms of what fits their needs. And if they have a low reference price, a low price on the software is part of what will meet their needs.

CUSTOMER CHOICES AMONG BRANDS

It's difficult to pinpoint why some customers respond favorably to a marketing mix and others don't. But understanding the needs of the different segments and then seeing the different marketing mix possibilities will provide some insights. Customers do look for products that have the features they want at the right price. But other factors also motivate purchase of a particular brand of software.

The amount of attention that a dealer devotes to the brand may make a difference too. Some customers are uncertain about what they want or may not know very much about the different brands available. A dealer's salesperson who is knowledgeable about a particular brand and able to demonstrate its features may be the deciding factor in completing the sale. Furthermore, some customers prefer to buy from the traditional dealers—and others prefer the discounters, perhaps because it's easier for them to find the product on the

Internet than it is to go to a local store. Either way, a customer is more likely to buy a brand that is available from a preferred type of dealer.

Brand awareness is important too. Advertising helps make customers aware of a brand. A customer may insist on a familiar brand—but be indifferent to one that is unfamiliar.

CONCLUSION

This report reviews the current state of the broad market in which you compete. It explains how your firm got to where it is today. It discusses the nature of the competition you face. It also highlights a number of potential opportunities—by identifying more homogeneous market segments and providing information that may help in developing better marketing mixes to meet the needs of target markets.

As consultants, we have tried to provide an objective report. We have avoided the temptation to inject much personal opinion—but rather have focused on the facts. In closing, however, we have a few recommendations to share.

We think that you, as the new marketing manager, have a real opportunity to do a better job than your predecessor did in selecting a target market and blending the 4Ps. The current head-to-head competition gives no one a competitive advantage. It appears that each competitor has pretty much followed the others. No firm seems to be doing an especially effective job of differentiating its offering to provide superior customer value to some specific market segment(s).

It may also be time to take a broader look at the product-market. Your firm now has a single product. There may be an opportunity to expand your product line to better meet the needs of the target market. In addition, your arrangement with the microchip producer allows you to develop a product that most other companies can't offer. Of course, you might face competition from your three primary rivals who have similar arrangements with the microchip maker. But, even so, that is less competition than many producers of computer accessories face. Of course, significant resources will be needed for your firm to develop any additional product—so any decision in that area will certainly need the approval of the firm's president.

We hope that this report has been helpful. We wish you the best of success with your new responsibilities. If Market-Views, Inc. can be of further assistance in the future, please call on us.

3. Marketing Department Responsibilities

Note: Before the previous marketing manager retired, the president asked him to summarize the marketing department's responsibilities—and review other relevant information that might be helpful to a new marketing manager. This chapter is the text of the memorandum prepared by the previous marketing manager.

INTRODUCTION

As marketing manager, you are in charge of planning marketing activities, implementing your plans, and controlling them. You play an important role in strategic planning—because you are heavily involved in matching the firm's resources to its market opportunities.

Much of your time will be spent developing a marketing plan. So this memo focuses on strategy decision areas that need to be included in your plan. But it also deals with implementing and controlling the plans you make. Objectives should set the course of your planning, so that is a good place to start.

OBJECTIVES

Your basic objectives are to use the resources of the firm wisely to meet target customer needs and contribute to the firm's profit. The time period is important here. Building long-term profitability sometimes requires that you spend money that results in lower short-term profits—or even losses. This does not mean that you can take losses lightly. Ultimately, the firm must earn profits to survive. And, if other competing firms continually earn higher profits, it may be difficult to attract investors and the resources the firm needs.

These objectives are general. You will want to set other, more specific objectives. That way, you will know when your marketing strategy is on course— or if it needs to be changed.

Your objectives should be realistic. The firm does not have unlimited resources—and it doesn't make sense for the marketing department to develop a plan that requires money the firm doesn't have.

RESOURCES

The firm has many talented employees. This is important to you. It means that the voice control programmers, engineers, and designers can develop the products you think will meet customers' needs. The firm also has the equipment and facilities to produce and distribute the products. But there are limits to these resources—and how much you can spend on a marketing strategy.

To make certain that there is enough money to operate the firm, the president sets a budget for each department for each year. You get your budget before you develop your marketing plan for the next year.

The president has more money to spend when profits are good. So a successful marketing strategy will lead to a higher budget. But, don't expect the president to give you a budget equal to all of the profit you generate; after all, other areas need budgets too. Further, the president knows that you need enough money to do a good job even if profits have been down. In fact, the firm gets data from a trade association on marketing spending by competing firms. The president analyzes this data—to be certain that you get a large enough budget to develop a competitive strategy. In general, I recommend that you spend all of the budget that is allocated to you. If you use the money wisely, you should be able to leverage your spending into even greater revenue. But, don't spend foolishly just to use up the money; remember that expenses must be paid before profits start to accumulate!

Once in the past, the marketing department appealed to the president to increase the budget amount—because we thought we had a sensible way to spend the money. At that time, the president did not grant our request, but he said that he did appreciate the accompanying proposal that explained how we wanted to spend the money and the results expected. The president's memo indicated that he would take the budget matter under consideration and that we would be told if there was enough money to entertain special budget requests. The memo also said that the president was giving consideration to authorizing a discretionary reserve fund. If the president authorizes a reserve fund, you would be able to spend against that fund, save it to spend in a later period, or simply leave it for an emergency. At any rate, the president will let you know if anything changes on the budget front. Unless you hear something different, you should manage your spending so that it doesn't exceed your budget.

The firm has developed planning forms (and decision support software) that make this easy. Although budget planning is not difficult, it is important. Thus, additional information about specific budget expenses will be given later in this memo. In addition, the computer programs discussed in Appendix A are a help.

Remember that a smart strategy need not be a high-cost strategy. Some target markets can be served well even with a low-cost marketing mix. Others might require a costly marketing mix but still be profitable. The focus of the marketing department is not on the budget per se—but rather spending the budget to best match the available resources to market opportunities. That requires careful selection of target markets—and skillful blending of the marketing mix to improve the customer value offered. You will be able to do a better job in these areas if you know the strategy decision areas over which you have control.

PRODUCT

The firm already has an established product—and a completely new product can't be developed and marketed without the president's authorization. But that doesn't mean that you can't modify the firm's established product to better meet the needs of target customers. To the contrary, it is likely that over time you will need to refine the product because changes in customer preferences and competitors offerings are likely to impact how satisfied customers are with your offering and what customer value it offers.

As marketing manager, you decide when and how product features should change. These decisions should be based on information about target market needs, costs of the features, and costs of changing those features. Obviously, what competitors are offering in the market is also relevant.

Features

You make decisions about three features that customers consider important: the number of special commands, the level of error protection, and the ease of learning. After you specify the features, R&D takes over to create the product.

But there are limits. Technology limitations prevent developers of the voice recognition instruction set for the VRD from creating a device with more than 20 special commands. And no one wants a device with fewer than five special commands. A testing lab supported by our industry trade association has developed a standard rating for levels of error protection. The rating can be between 1 and 10—where 1 is very low on error protection and 10 is high. Similarly, there is an accepted 1 to 10 industry rating for ease of learning. Thus, you specify the features of your product by deciding on the number of special commands (between 5 and 20) and the ratings (from 1 to 10) for the level of error protection and ease of learning.

Cost of R&D for Product Modification

The R&D people can in general modify the product quite quickly, within the limits discussed above. Further, experience shows that the number of special commands and the level of error protection can be decreased without cost. But the cost of other R&D product modifications can be substantial—especially if large changes are required in a single planning period. Further, these R&D and new-product development costs are charged to the marketing budget when they are incurred—so they must be considered in developing the marketing plan.

The cost accounting experts in the firm have figured out a simple and accurate way to estimate the R&D cost of modifying each feature. Their approach is summarized in the table below:

► Estimating the R&D Costs for Product Modifications

FEATURE	Feasible Range	Cost to Change Level from Previous Period	
		To Decrease Level	*To Increase Level*
Special Commands	5-20	no cost	$8,000 x (change) x (change)
Error Protection	1-10	no cost	$5,000 x (change) x (change)
Ease of Learning	1-10	$3,000 x (change)	$3,000 x (change) x (change)

In this table, the term change refers to the difference in the level of the feature from one period to the next. The total product modification cost is the sum of the costs to change individual features.

Let's consider an example. The table below shows the costs to modify a brand which in the previous period had 6 special commands, an error protection rating of 4, and an ease of use rating of 3 to create a "new" brand with 8 special commands, an error protection rating of 3, and an ease of learning rating of 5.

► Example of R&D Product Modification Costs

FEATURE	LEVEL		CHANGE	COST
	Old Product	*New Product*		
Special Commands	6	8	+2	$8,000 x 2 x 2 =$32,000
Error Protection	4	3	-1	no cost for decrease =$0
Ease of Learning	3	5	+2	$3,000 x 2 x 2 =$12,000

Thus, to make the changes described above the total product modification cost would be $32,000 + $0 + $12,000 = $44,000.

Note that it costs more if R&D must make big changes in a short period of time. For example, to increase the number of Special Commands from 6 to 10 in a single period would be $8,000 x 4 x 4 = $128,000. By contrast, to increase from 6 to 8 in one period and then increase from 8 to 10 in the following period would only be $64,000 (i.e., as shown in the table above, $32,000 for each period). Thus, it is wise to consider whether the added R&D costs to make really big changes in a short period of time are really justified, or if planning incremental changes over a longer period is more sensible. Unfortunately, there are no easy answers in this area. Sometimes the advantages of speed in giving the market what it wants justifies the expense, but that may depend on what kinds of changes competitors make, and how fast they make them.

Regardless of how big a product change you want to make, the cost of the R&D for the required product modification is charged to your budget in the period when the changes are made. Further, the total product modification cost stays the same regardless of how much you sell in that period. So, if you make a big,

32

Mason & Perreault

expensive change but the market reaction is unfavorable, you pay for your mistake not only with lost revenue but also with out-of-pocket R&D expense. The other side of the coin is that there is no product modification cost when there is no change in product features for a period. Even with no product modification there is still risk. You may lose customers and sales to a competitor with a new, improved product.

You can continue to modify your brand in the future if that is necessary to implement your strategy. However, product modification costs occur each time you change the product—even if the features are returned to the level of a previous year. For example, you might reduce the number of special commands one year and then add them back the next year. Although the total number of commands would be the same, there would be a cost to modify the design to include the commands again.

All product modifications are completed before production for the year starts. Thus, all units sold during the period have the new features. This is another reason why it is so important to have your plan in by the deadline specified by the president. If the plan is late, there may not be time to modify the product before production begins.

Unit Production Cost

The production department reports that the level on each feature directly affects the unit production cost. Specifically,

Unit production cost = $4 x (Number of special commands) +
$3 x (Error protection rating) +
$2 x (Ease of learning rating).

Thus, your unit cost can vary from $25 to $130 depending on the features of the brand. The cost of actually producing units is not charged to the marketing department budget. But production cost is certainly an important consideration. A product that is costly to produce may require a price that is too high for the target market. And customers may not want—or buy—a product with the wrong combination of features. Further, the cost of goods sold for the period—along with other expenses—is subtracted from sales revenue to arrive at profit contribution.

Experts in the production department have been studying ways to reduce production costs. In a report, they said that they may be able to achieve economies of scale as the firm's cumulative production quantity increases. Specifically, they estimated that they should be able to reduce unit production costs by about 3 percent for each additional 100,000 units the firm produces—although the savings might ultimately taper off. However, the potential cost savings depend on making changes in the production equipment, and the V.P. of production and the V.P. of finance are still debating the wisdom of purchasing the equipment. However, the president will make an announcement if the equipment is purchased. Unless there is such an announcement, you should continue to use the unit cost estimates overviewed above.

Customer Service

While our basic product is the device we sell, many customers expect to be able to get after-the-sale customer service if they have a question. They think of the availability of technical help as part of the product they buy. So customer service seems to be an important issue. And the service level a firm provides is getting more attention in the press. Firms that haven't handled it well have faced bad publicity, negative word-of-mouth among customers, and a backlash in sales.

Some customers look to our website for customer support, and some call our customer service phone number. As is the practice of our competitors, we leave it to the customer to pay for the phone call to ask a question—so telephone line charges are not an expense. But the marketing department must decide how much money to spend on staff to support the customer service queries that come in via the website or over the telephone lines.

It appears that most customer service requests come from new customers—within the first year after they have purchased our VRD. And for the most part the questions are easy to answer. Thus, we have been able to staff the phones and website with part-time employees whom we schedule to work when the requests and calls are heaviest; they can always turn the tough questions—or the real problems—over to one of the engineers or device programmers.

At any rate, the money spent to support customer service comes out of the marketing department budget. It makes sense to take a careful look at spending in this area. A mistake may certainly hurt us; but it's not clear whether doing a really good job can help us.

PLACE

In developing your marketing plan, you must decide on the level of distribution intensity that you want in each channel of distribution. Operationally, you can think of distribution intensity as the percentage of available dealers in each channel that you want to stock and sell your software.

In an absolute sense, the level of distribution intensity (market exposure) in a channel may range from exclusive to selective to intensive—depending on the firm's marketing strategy. Exclusive distribution is selling through only one (or very few) dealers in each market—and implies that you would expect salespeople to call on a relatively small percentage of the available dealers in a channel. Selective distribution is selling through those dealers who will give your product special attention; it implies that the sales reps may call on a mid-range percentage of the available dealers in a channel. And intensive distribution is selling through all responsible and suitable dealers in a channel, although as a practical matter it probably would be too difficult and expensive to achieve 100 percent coverage.

Because the dealers in the two channels are quite different, the level of distribution intensity in one channel has no direct influence on the level of distribution intensity in the other. Therefore you may want different levels of distribution intensity in the different channels. In fact, if you wish you can elect to stop selling in one of the channels. We've considered that in the past, but so far have not had time to study whether it might be a good idea.

In spite of the conflict that we created selling direct earlier, it does not appear that our move to distribute through two different channels has reopened that can of worms. To the contrary, the traditional full-service dealers seem resolved to the fact that the Internet discounters have become a fact of life. So, instead of just discounting prices, full-service dealers have worked to improve their service, warranty coverage, and take whatever other steps they can to differentiate the value they offer customers.

In your marketing plan, use a rating of 0 (i.e., zero percent of the dealers) if you don't want to use dealers in a certain channel at all. Otherwise, use a rating between the extremes of 1 percent of the dealers (extremely exclusive) and 100 percent of the dealers (extremely intensive) to indicate the distribution intensity level you desire. Because this "percentage of dealers" approach has been used in the firm for some time now, it is a concise way to summarize what type of distribution you're planning.

Keep in mind that the level of distribution intensity you desire for your strategy may not be achieved if it's not consistent with other parts of your strategy, including how you handle promotion.

PROMOTION

Personal Selling

The sales force plays a key role in recruiting new dealers, getting orders from dealers, and providing them with support and training. Because of differences in dealers, sales reps specialize by channel.

The marketing manager is responsible for deciding how many sales reps the firm needs in total—and how many are assigned to each channel. This is an important strategy decision area. Decisions here must consider the distribution intensity level in each channel. Achieving intensive distribution typically requires more personal selling effort—more sales reps—than selective distribution. Similarly, selective distribution requires more sales reps than exclusive distribution. Too little sales coverage in channels will hurt sales and relations with dealers. Too much coverage might help sales some—but if the added sales don't justify the increased sales force costs it will hurt profits.

Personal selling salaries—$20,000 a year per rep—are charged to the marketing budget. Each sales rep also earns 5 percent commission on all sales to dealers. Since the total commission amount varies with the quantity sold, sales commissions are not paid out of the marketing department budget. But they are an expense so they directly affect contribution to profit.

The commission percent is currently set by company policy—to keep sales compensation in line with pay for other jobs in the company. However, the director of the human resources department has acknowledged that the marketing department might be able to motivate sales reps better if it could set the commission rate. The reps also pay attention to commissions that other firms pay. We had a meeting with the president on this issue, and it is being considered. I assume that the president will let you know if marketing area responsibility in this area is to be expanded.

New sales reps can be hired as needed to expand the sales force. Beyond the $20,000 a year salary, there is no direct charge for hiring a new rep. However, in this company new reps spend about 20 percent of the first year in training. So, in the first year, they are only 80 percent as productive as an experienced rep.

You can fire sales reps (but not all of them) if you want to reduce the size of the sales force. But you must make firing decisions carefully. It disrupts a rep's life to lose his or her job. Furthermore, the company gives each fired rep $5,000 in severance pay, and the $5,000 must be paid from the marketing department budget.

Sometimes you can avoid hiring or firing by reassigning a rep from one channel to the other. There is no cost to reassign a rep. And because experienced reps seem to adjust to the new channel situation quickly, there is no real loss in selling effectiveness.

The president of our firm feels very strongly that sales reps play an important role in developing good long-term relations with dealers. To ensure good relations with dealers, the president has instructed that sales reps spend 10 percent of their time on non-selling or support activities. These activities include explaining the technical details of the product, training the dealers' salespeople, and generally building goodwill with the dealers. Clearly, firms that have ignored these support activities in the past have lost important dealers. Even so, it's hard to tell if 10 percent is the right allocation for support tasks.

Advertising

Advertising is used to inform customers about VRD capabilities and benefits in general. It's also used to promote the strengths of the firm's brand relative to competing brands. How much to spend on advertising is an important strategy decision. Advertising costs are paid from the marketing budget. The firm works with an advertising agency that helps develop the actual ads and works out the details of what media to use. The agency also has in-house specialists who do a good job of leveraging advertising materials developed primarily for other media so that they can be used to enhance the promotional value of our website.

The ad agency argues that the amount spent on advertising impacts advertising effectiveness. However, the ad agency cannot say exactly how large a sales volume will result from a given advertising budget. This is because customers respond to the whole marketing mix, not just advertising. But the ad agency has provided some general guidelines.

First, advertising impact depends not only on your firm's level of advertising but also on what competitors spend on advertising. Very low levels of advertising—below some threshold level—will have little impact. The advertising message will be lost among the clutter of competitors' ads. But, at the other extreme, there is an upper limit on the sales that advertising can generate. Money spent on advertising that approaches or exceeds that saturation level is wasted.

This is a dynamic market. Advertising has the greatest effect in the year it's done. But some benefit may carry over to the next year or future years. Advertising impact may also vary depending on the type of advertising that's done. The agency works with the firm to select the best type of advertising for the money available. Marketing department decisions in that area are usually based on what competitors are doing and on the stage in the product life cycle, as well as the objectives to be accomplished.

PRICE

Legal Environment

Price is an important strategy decision area. You set the wholesale price—the price paid by your dealers. At present, the legal department in the firm requires that you charge all dealers the same price. However, the firm's lawyers are studying the laws in this area. They think that it may be legal to charge a different wholesale price to dealers in the two channels since they provide different kinds of marketing functions. Until the lawyers decide, however, you must charge the same wholesale price in each channel.

Price Affects Demand

Dealers set the retail price—but you should consider the likely retail price when you set the wholesale price. The retail price will affect the quantity demanded by the target market. Some segments of the market are more price-sensitive than others.

You can easily calculate the likely retail price because dealers use customary markup percents—50 percent in Channel 1 and 35 percent in Channel 2. The way to do the calculation is:

$$(Likely) \ retail \ price = (Wholesale \ Price \times 100) / (100 - Markup \ percent)$$

You are free to change the wholesale price from one year to the next. But substantial price changes from year to year may confuse customers and dealers.

Price Should Cover Costs

The revenue you earn is equal to the wholesale price times the quantity sold. The price should be high enough to cover unit production costs and leave enough to contribute to other expenses (including sales commissions) and profit. Planning is important here.

As discussed earlier, you can estimate unit production costs based on the product features you're planning. Other costs to consider are those that are charged to the marketing department budget. Most of these have been covered earlier. As a convenient summary, however, they are listed below:

► **Summary of Costs Charged to Marketing Department Budget**

Product modification costs (if any),
Customer service costs,
Sales force salaries and severance pay,
Advertising expense, and
Marketing research expense.

Marketing research expense depends on how many marketing research reports you buy. Marketing research is covered next.

MARKETING RESEARCH

Marketing research can be an important source of information about your target market, how well your marketing plan is working, and what competitors are doing. Some marketing research information is available free from secondary sources—including reports in trades magazines, data available on the Internet, and studies by the industry trade associations. Much information is also available at no cost from the firm's marketing information system (MIS). In addition, an outside marketing research firm sells a variety of useful marketing research reports. Examples of the different reports are provided in the next chapter, but they are briefly described below.

Information Available at No Cost

► *Industry Sales Report*

Each year, the industry trade association compiles an Industry Sales Report and provides a copy to each firm in the industry. The report summarizes the total unit sales and the total (retail) dollar sales for each brand. It also reports the market shares for each firm based on both unit sales and dollar sales. Moreover, it gives total unit sales and total (retail) dollar sales for each distribution channel.

► *Product Features and Prices Report*

Sales reps are instructed to report back to the firm the features of all brands on the market and the retail price for each brand in each channel. This information is organized in the firm's marketing information system and is summarized at the end of the year in a Product Features and Prices Report.

► *Marketing Activity Report*

Over time, the market research department collects information about each competitor's promotion blend. Competitors try to keep their plans secret—so it's impossible to get this information in advance. However, much of it is quickly available from advertising media and trade associations, dealers, trade publications, and even competitors' websites and reports to stockholders. This information is compiled in the firm's MIS to produce the Marketing Activity Report. It includes summaries—for each firm—of spending on advertising, sales force size and commission rate, and any sales promotion activity. This timely information is fairly accurate and thus gives an idea of what competitors are doing in the market.

Reports from an Outside Marketing Research Firm

An outside marketing research firm specializes in ongoing studies of the software market in which you compete. Results from its studies are summarized in six reports. The reports are available each year. But the marketing research firm requires advance payment. You can purchase any report or combination of reports. The costs for the different reports vary. The title of each report and its cost is listed in the table below.

▶ Costs of Different Marketing Research Reports

Report Number	Title of Report	Cost
1	Market Share by Segment (all brands)	$15,000
2	Market Share by Channel (all brands)	$12,000
3	Consumer Preference Study	$30,000
4	Marketing Effectiveness Report	$25,000
5	Sales by Segment by Channel (firm's brand)	$15,000
6	Customer Shopping Habits Survey	$7,000

A brief description of each report follows—and samples appear in the next chapter.

▶ Market Share by Segment

This report gives the market shares (based on units sold) for each brand in each market segment. It also gives the total unit sales for each segment.

▶ Market Share by Channel

This report summarizes the market shares, based on units sold, for each brand in each distribution channel. The report also includes total unit sales for each channel.

▶ Consumer Preference Study

This study summarizes the results of a sample survey of actual and potential customers from the various market segments. Customers indicate their most preferred (or ideal) level for each product feature. The numbers in the report are the average values reported by members of each segment.

Although representative customers are surveyed, the sample estimates may not be exact for the whole population. The research firm says that the results are accurate to within 10 percent of the true values for the different market segments.

This report also gives a price range for each segment. This range merely indicates the prices that members of the different segments typically expect to pay for a VRD.

▶ *Marketing Effectiveness Report*

This report summarizes the results of survey research on the effectiveness of your customer service as well as your advertising and personal selling decisions—both in an absolute sense and relative to competitors.

One measure of advertising effectiveness is the proportion of customers who are aware of your brand. This measure is reported as a Brand Awareness Index ranging from 0.0 to 1.0. A higher index indicates greater awareness (familiarity). In practice, however, an index greater than .9 is very rare.

There is also a measure based on the customer service the firm provides. It is reported as a percentage rating, where a lower percentage suggests lower satisfaction with the service provided. This firm-specific measure can be compared with a measure of the average rating for the overall industry, which is also provided.

Additional indexes indicate the effectiveness of the firm's efforts in each of the channels of distribution. The marketing research firm develops the Sales Rep Workload Index by studying how sales reps spend their time and how well satisfied dealers are with the service they receive from a rep. An index of less than 100 percent indicates that sales reps can satisfactorily handle all their accounts and could potentially call on more dealers. On the other hand, an index that exceeds 100 percent indicates that sales reps are overloaded and are trying to call on more dealers than they can effectively service.

The Dealer Satisfaction Index is basically a summary measure of what dealers think about the quality and effectiveness of your sales force as well as any trade promotion assistance they receive. This index generally varies above and below 1.00. If it is less that 1.00, it suggests that dealers are not satisfied with some aspects of your promotion blend, at least relative to what competitors are doing. If it is greater than 1.00, this may be an area of competitive advantage. However, this advantage may be coming at the cost of greater spending on sales effort or promotion in the channel.

The Channel Strength ("Push") Index is basically a summary measure of the overall "push" that your brand gets in consumer purchase decisions from dealers in the channel of distribution. It takes into consideration the number of dealers who are carrying your brand and how much effort they are willing to put behind it—relative to competing brands. Like the Brand Awareness Index, the values on this index range between 0.0 and 1.00; however, in practice values over .80 are rare.

The research firm will not sell all of this detailed information for competing brands. But the report does provide some summary information. It gives the number of competitors with a lower index and the number of competitors with an index that is the same or greater. This report is expensive—but it does provide insights about your marketing strengths and weaknesses.

▶ **Detailed Sales Analysis**

This report details the number of units of your brand sold to each market segment through each channel. It can be very useful to see if the intended target market is buying the product—and, if so, from what dealers.

▶ **Customer Shopping Habits Survey**

This survey is used to determine the percentage of time that customers in the different segments shop in Channel 1 compared with Channel 2. The research is based on a sample of customers, and because of "sampling error" the results may not be exact for the whole population of customers. However, the market research firm says that the sample estimates are within 5 percent of the true values for the full population of customers.

Marketing Research—Benefits versus Costs

Much useful market research information is available. You should weigh the potential benefits of this information against the cost. Before deciding to buy a report, think about how you will use the information. Further, think about how the information can be used in combination with other data to give you additional insights. Advance planning for marketing research can lead to a more sensible use of your marketing budget.

FORECASTING DEMAND

It is the responsibility of the marketing department to forecast demand for the coming year. This forecast may be based on many different kinds of information—past sales trends, estimates of target market potential and growth, juries of executive judgment (for example, about what competitors are likely to do), and market research about customers' preferences. Of course, the forecast must consider how well the marketing mix meets target customers' needs.

Developing a good forecast is important for several reasons. You will need a forecast of what you expect to sell to evaluate your marketing plan—to estimate expected revenues and profit/contribution. But there is an even more immediate reason. The production department uses the estimate of demand as a production order quantity. This is an important decision for marketing management.

The Production Order Quantity

Lead times to produce VRDs are short. As a result, the production department is able to increase production as much as 20 percent above your production order quantity to satisfy unexpected demand. It can also reduce the actual production quantity by up to 20 percent if the product does not sell as expected. This gives quite a bit of flexibility.

However, if the forecast is off by more than 20 percent, problems arise. If demand is greater than that limit, sales will be lost—perhaps to a competitor with better product availability. If demand is more than 20 percent lower than the production order quantity, there will be excess inventory of out-of-date VRDs at the end of the year. Selling this inventory in bulk at Internet auction sites would just dump it back into our market--and cannibalize sales of our updated device. So, instead, it is transferred to an export agent for sale in a foreign market. This involves added costs—tariffs, agent fees, and shipping—and it isn't possible to recover the full unit production cost on these units. Therefore, if the firm overproduces in any year, the marketing department budget is charged. The charge is 15 percent of the production cost for all units shipped to overseas markets.

CONCLUSION

This memorandum overviews the major strategy decision areas that must be considered in developing the marketing plan. It also reviews issues that should be considered in making decisions in each of these areas.

One final point should be emphasized. Each year, after the marketing plan has been developed, it must be submitted to the president for final approval. So that the president can quickly overview the full set of decisions you've made, these decisions are to be submitted on a special summary form. Sometimes the president asks for other supporting documentation. The president will tell you what you need to do in that area. But it is very important to meet the deadline for submitting your plan. If you miss the deadline, it may not be possible to make desired product changes in time or to meet production schedules. Other serious problems may also arise. In fact, if the plan is late the president may have no alternative except to simply authorize a continuation of the plan you submitted in the previous period. Obviously, that wouldn't leave the president with a good impression of the people in the marketing department. Therefore, meeting the deadline is critical.

4. Submitting the Marketing Plan

Note: Depending on the scope of your responsibilities, you will be told to read this chapter or to read Chapter 5 instead. At this point, you don't need to read both.

The president requests that you submit a form summarizing your annual plan. The president instructed a staff assistant to provide you with a copy of the form and any related information you might need. In addition, the president asked the assistant to provide you with a copy of the firm's most recent financial summary and examples of other reports that are available annually. This chapter is the material prepared by the president's assistant.

MARKETING PLAN DECISIONS FORM

After you develop your annual marketing plan, the president wants you to submit a summary form that overviews your decisions. In our firm we usually ask you to submit an electronic version of the form (which you create with the computer program described in Appendix A) as well as a paper version for verification purposes; however, in separate communication we'll update you on the details of getting the completed form (in paper format, computer file format, or both) to us.

The previous marketing manager has already reviewed the strategy decision areas covered by the form (see previous chapter). But—for your reference in completing the form—a concise summary of his major points is provided on the next page. There is also a copy of the Marketing Plan Decisions Form (Exhibit 4A). In fact, this is the completed form submitted by the previous marketing manager at the beginning of this past year. It summarizes the marketing plan decisions he made last year.

The form and notes are simple and clear—so they do not need further explanation here. The president will set the deadline for you to submit your decisions. The president will also tell you if you need to submit any other information along with the summary.

Guide to the Marketing Plan Decisions Form (Level 1)

Distribution Intensity:	The desired distribution intensity level (percent of dealers) must be specified for each channel. The minimum value is 0, implying no distribution in that channel. Otherwise, the percentage should be between the extremes of 1 percent (extremely exclusive distribution) and a maximum of 100 percent (indicating extremely intensive distribution).
Number of Sales Reps:	The number of sales representatives must be specified for each channel. Each sales rep earns $20,000 per year in salary. Each sales rep that is fired receives $5,000 in severance pay.
Customer Service:	The dollar amount that you spend on customer service must be greater than or equal to zero.
Brand name:	The brand name may be up to 10 characters long. It is used for identification on reports, and thus should not be changed once it is set in the first period.
BRAND FEATURES: --Number of special commands	The number of special commands must be between 5 and 20.
--Error Protection	The error protection rating must be between 1 and 10. A higher rating corresponds to greater error protection.
--Ease of Learning	This rating must be between 1 and 10. A higher rating corresponds to greater ease of learning.
Production Order Quantity:	The production order must be greater than or equal to 100. It should be within 20 percent of your forecast of demand for your brand to avoid inventory stock-outs if you underproduce, or to avoid transfer charges resulting from excess inventory if you overproduce.
Advertising Dollars:	Advertising spending must be greater than or equal to zero.
Wholesale Price:	The wholesale price must be between $75 and $250. Your management will not accept a wholesale price below $75, and a wholesale price greater than $250 leads to retail prices higher than any consumers are willing to pay.

Marketing Research Reports:	You may purchase any of the following reports:	Price for Report
	1. Market Share by Segment (all brands)	$15,000
	2. Market Share by Channel (all brands)	$12,000
	3. Consumer Preference Study	$30,000
	4. Marketing Effectiveness Report	$25,000
	5. Detailed Sales Analysis (own brand)	$15,000
	6. Customer Shopping Habits Survey	$7,000

Exhibit 4A: Marketing Plan Decisions Form-Level 1

```
Marketing Plan Decisions - Level 1
```

General

Channel 1   Channel 2

| 30 | | 30 | Distribution intensity (% of dealers)
| 10 | | 10 | Number of sales reps (0-100)

| $92,500 | Customer service budget
($0-$9,999,999)

Marketing Research

Product 1
1. Share by segment ☑
2. Share by channel ☑
3. Preferences ☐
4. Effectiveness ☑
5. Segment by channel ☑
6. Shopping habits ☐

Industry and Firm

Product 1

| FirmX | Brand name (8 letters)

Features
| 8 | Special Commands (5-20)
| 3 | Error Protection (1-10)
| 3 | Ease of Learning (1-10)
| 25,000 | Production Order Quantity (> 99)
| $250,000 | Advertising Spending

| $95 | Wholesale Price
($75-$250)

Note: This sample of the form is completed with the decisions made by the previous marketing manager in the last period.

Blank copies of this form appear at the end of the manual.

FEEDBACK FOR CONTROL AND PLANNING

At the end of each year, you will receive important feedback about the performance of your plan. You'll get the following reports:

1. annual financial summary (including your budget for the next period),
2. a production summary,
3. the industry sales report,
4. the industry product features and prices report,
5. the industry marketing activity report, and
6. any additional marketing research reports you have purchased.

These reports should be used for control purposes—and as a basis for future planning and marketing decisions. Exhibit 4B—which starts on page 48 and continues for four pages—provides copies of the latest set of reports (i.e., from the previous period).

Please study these reports before developing your plan. They show the results produced by the marketing plan decisions submitted last year by the previous marketing manager (see Exhibit 4A). They also summarize the firm's current financial position, your budget for the next period, and other important information.

ANNUAL FINANCIAL SUMMARY

The Financial Summary is clearly labeled and does not need much additional explanation. A few comments, however, may be helpful.

The unit cost, $47.00, is what it cost per unit to produce a VRD with the features specified by the previous marketing manager.

Gross sales is the revenue received from sales to dealers. You can confirm that gross sales is equal to the units sold multiplied by the wholesale price charged to dealers.

The cost of goods sold is computed by multiplying the number of units sold by the unit cost. (Note: some accountants refer to cost of goods sold by some other name, such as cost of sales. This firm has been using the term cost of goods sold for some time, so that term has been retained for consistency).

The gross margin is the money left after cost of goods sold is subtracted from gross sales. The gross margin is used to cover other costs and contribute to profits.

The various expense items are the costs of the marketing plan submitted by the previous marketing manager. You may wish to crosscheck these expenses against the Marketing Plan Decisions Form he submitted.

Net contribution to profit (or loss) is what is left after subtracting expenses from the gross margin.

At the bottom of the financial summary is the budget that the president has set aside for the marketing department for next year. As you can see, you have up to $984,000 to spend. Based on trade association data, this amount represents about 25 percent of what all four firms in this industry will spend on marketing.

Finally, keep in mind that in this summary report each figure shown has been rounded off to a whole number. However, calculations done for the report are done before numbers are rounded off. As a result, for example, the total expenses amount shown in the report might be a dollar or two higher or lower than what you would get by adding up the rounded-off numbers.

PRODUCTION SUMMARY

The Production Summary shows requested production—the production order quantity submitted by the previous marketing manager based on his forecast of demand. Actual production was slightly higher—to meet demand for the 25,151 units actually sold. There was no excess inventory at the end of the year, so there were no transfer charges for overseas sales.

MARKETING RESEARCH REPORTS

The various marketing research reports have already been described (see Chapter 3). But Exhibit 4B provides the actual reports for this year.

Two of the marketing research reports in Exhibit 4B warrant comment. First, the firm did not purchase the Consumer Preferences Study (report number 3) last year. However, the firm has purchased it in the past—and the tables shows a range of estimates based on past reports. However, if you buy this report from the marketing research firm in the future, you will get a current report that should be more precise (within the error due to survey sampling) with estimates of average consumer preferences for different features (by segment).

Second, the Customer Shopping Habits Survey (report number 6) has never been purchased by the firm, and as a result the information found in this report is not available to the firm. However, the sample shows the general format used in this report. If you buy this report from the marketing research firm in the future, you will get a completed report that shows the proportion of consumers from different segments who shop in each of the channels.

Exhibit 4B: Company Report for Previous Period

```
*************** Financial Summary ***************

FIRM X                   Channel 1        Channel 2          Total
-------
Units Sold                   14074            11077          25151
Wholesale Price             $95.00           $95.00
Unit Cost                   $47.00           $47.00

Gross Sales             $1,337,030       $1,052,315     $2,389,345
Cost of Goods Sold        $661,478         $520,619     $1,182,097
Transfer Charges                                                $0
Gross Margin                                            $1,207,248


Expenses
Advertising                                               $250,000
Sales Force -Salary       $200,000         $200,000       $400,000
            -Firing Costs                                       $0
            -Commission     $66,852          $52,616       $119,468
Customer Service                                           $92,500
R&D for Product Modifications                                   $0
Marketing Research                                         $67,000
Total Expenses                                            $928,968

Net Contribution (Loss)                                   $278,280
```

Budget for Next Period: $984,000   (25% of Industry Total)

```
************** Production Summary ***************

        Requested     Actual        Units    Inventory    Unit
Brand   Production    Production     Sold     Transferred  Cost
_____   _____    _____     _____    _____   ____

FIRM X    25000         25151        25151         0       $47.
```

Exhibit 4B (continued)

```
****************** Industry Sales Report ***************
```

VRD Brand	Unit Sales	Market Share (Units)	$ Sales	Market Share ($ Sales)
FIRM 1	25,151	0.250	$4,292,964	0.250
FIRM 2	25,151	0.250	$4,292,964	0.250
FIRM 3	25,151	0.250	$4,292,964	0.250
FIRM 4	25,151	0.250	$4,292,964	0.250
Total	100,604		$17,171,854	

Channel	Unit Sales	$ Sales
1	56,296	$10,696,240
2	44,308	$6,475,614

```
************ Product Features & Prices Report ***********
```

VRD Brand	Special Commands	Error Protection	Ease of Learning	Average Retail Price Channel 1	Average Retail Price Channel 2
FIRM 1	8	3	3	$190.00	$146.15
FIRM 2	8	3	3	$190.00	$146.15
FIRM 3	8	3	3	$190.00	$146.15
FIRM 4	8	3	3	$190.00	$146.15

```
*************** Marketing Activity Report ***************
               (Data Reported Is for Period 0)
```

	FIRM 1	FIRM 2	FIRM 3	FIRM 4
Advertising Dollars	$250,000	$250,000	$250,000	$250,000
Advertising Type				
Sales Promotion				
-Channel 1	$0	$0	$0	$0
-Channel 2	$0	$0	$0	$0
Number of Sales Reps				
-Channel 1	10	10	10	10
-Channel 2	10	10	10	10
Commission Rate	5%	5%	5%	5%
Customer Service	$92,500	$92,500	$92,500	$92,500

Exhibit 4B (continued)

```
********** Report 1: Market Share By Segment ***********
```

Segment:	Students	Home	Assistants	Creators	Managers	Parents
Brand	-------	-------	-------	-------	-------	-------

FIRM 1	0.250	0.250	0.250	0.250	0.250	0.250
FIRM 2	0.250	0.250	0.250	0.250	0.250	0.250
FIRM 3	0.250	0.250	0.250	0.250	0.250	0.250
FIRM 4	0.250	0.250	0.250	0.250	0.250	0.250
Total Sales (in Units)	20,028	15,084	25,104	10,240	22,056	8,092

```
********** Report 2: Market Share By Channel **********
```

Brand	Channel 1	Channel 2
-----	---------	---------
FIRM 1	0.250	0.250
FIRM 2	0.250	0.250
FIRM 3	0.250	0.250
FIRM 4	0.250	0.250
Total Sales (in Units)	56,296	44,308

```
******* Report 3: Average Customer Preferences ********
```

Segment	Special Commands	Error Protection	Ease of Learning	Price Range
-------	--------	----------	---------	-----------
Students	10-13	2-4	1-3	low
Home	7-10	2-4	6-8	low
Assistants	10-13	6-8	6-8	high
Creators	12-15	2-4	4-6	high
Managers	13-16	6-8	2-4	high
Parents	5-8	2-4	7-9	low

Mason & Perreault

Exhibit 4B (continued)

```
******* Report 4: Marketing Effectiveness Report ******
```

	Index	# of Competitors with Lower Index	# of Competitors with Equal or Higher Index
Awareness - FIRM X	0.550	0	3
Customer Service			
Consumer Group Rating	100%		
Industry Average Rating	100%		
Channel 1:			
Sales Rep Workload Index	100%		
Dealer Satisfaction	0.815	0	3
Channel Strength ("Push")	0.500	0	3
Channel 2			
Sales Rep Workload Index	100%		
Dealer Satisfaction	1.043	0	3
Channel Strength ("Push")	.500	0	3

```
********** Report 5: Detailed Sales Analysis **********
```

Segment	Students	Home	Assistants	Creators	Managers	Parents
FIRM X						
-Channel 1	708	936	5,080	1,578	4,752	1,020
-Channel 2	4,299	2,835	1,196	982	762	1,003

```
**********Report 6: Customer Shopping Habitsª **********
```

Segment	Percent of Shopping in Channel 1	Percent of Shopping in Channel 2
Students	?	?
Home	?	?
Assistants	?	?
Creators	?	?
Managers	?	?
Parents	?	?

[a]Note: this report has not previously been purchased, which explains why the proportion of consumers in each segment shopping in each channel is not reported; however, the proportions would be reported if the current report is purchased.

5. Submitting an Expanded Marketing Plan

*Note: Depending on the scope of your responsibilities, you will be told to read Chapter 4 or to read this chapter instead. **Unless you are instructed otherwise, you don't need to read both.***

The president has decided to expand the responsibilities of the marketing department. In addition, the president wants you to submit a form summarizing your marketing plan. The president asked a staff assistant to prepare a memo to tell you what you need to do. The president also asked the assistant to provide you with a copy of the firm's most recent financial summary and examples of other reports that are available annually. This chapter is the material prepared by the president's assistant.

INTRODUCTION

Each year, the marketing manager submits a form summarizing key marketing plan decisions. The president has decided to ask for more detail on this form than has been requested in the past. In addition, the president has decided to expand marketing department responsibilities in several areas. This memo reviews these changes. In addition, a copy of the expanded Marketing Plan Decisions Form (Level 2) is included. Finally, several reports that give you important information about the firm and the results of last year's marketing plan are discussed.

EXPANDED RESPONSIBILITIES

Price

The legal department has recommended to the president that the marketing department be allowed to set different wholesale prices for dealers in the two channels. The firm's lawyers have concluded that this will not result in legal problems.

Promotion

▶ Personal Selling

The president has decided that the marketing department should be allowed to set the sales force commission percent—which company policy previously set at 5 percent of sales. A higher commission rate might increase sales rep motivation—but, of course, it is a selling expense that is subtracted from gross margin in arriving at profit contribution. The president has requested that the commission rate not exceed 15 percent—so that sales compensation does not get totally out of line with other pay rates in the firm.

In the past, the president has had a policy that sales reps spend approximately 10 percent of their time on support (non-selling) activities. However, the president is not certain that the policy makes sense. So, it is now a marketing department responsibility to decide, for each channel, what percent of a sales rep's time should be spent on support activities. This gives you new flexibility to make more effective use of the sales force. For example, you might conclude that spending more time in support activities will strengthen our relationships with members of our channel and result in better customer satisfaction and earnings. Conversely, you can even specify that sales reps spend no time on support activities if that is what you believe best fits your overall strategy. However, the president has directed that at least 50 percent of a sales rep's time be devoted to selling activities.

▶ Advertising

In the past, the marketing manager and the ad agency worked out the details of what advertising would be done. Only the dollar amount to be spent on advertising was reported to the president on the Marketing Plan Decisions Form. So that the president will have a better idea of how the money is going to be spent, please include information about the type of advertising you plan to use to achieve your marketing objectives. The president may ask for more supporting detail in some other form. But, to keep the planning form concise, you simply indicate on it which type of advertising you will be using: pioneering advertising, direct competitive advertising, indirect competitive advertising, reminder advertising, or corporate (institutional) advertising.

▶ Sales Promotion

In the past, the firm used sales promotion targeted at dealers only irregularly. Often no one spent much time considering sales promotion targeted at the trade when developing the marketing plan, and if sales promotion was used, it was paid for with special funds. To encourage more careful planning of sales (trade) promotion, the president has asked that your marketing plan indicate how much you will be spending on sales promotion in each channel. Also, please note that spending for sales (trade) promotion will now be charged to the marketing department budget.

Marketing Research

The office of the president has just received a letter from the outside marketing research firm that sells us the Consumer Preference Study (marketing research report 3). The letter explained that the research firm has developed a new "product positioning" study that might enable you to get a better idea of how well our VRD—and the products offered by competitors—are meeting the needs of different customer segments.

Specifically, the letter explains that the study uses a computerized approach called perceptual mapping to determine how closely our brand (and competitors' brands) matches customers' ideal brand in each of the different segments. The results of the research are provided in a simple table, where each row in the table represents one of the four competing products, and where each column represents one of the six key market segments. The entries in the table can be thought of as "distances" of each of the brands from each segment's ideal. Thus, a high number suggests a greater distance—and a brand that is not very similar to the segment's ideal. Conversely, a low number indicates a small distance, suggesting that a brand is quite similar to the segment's ideal. The marketing research firm says that it will not reveal the details of the proprietary procedure it uses to develop these summary measures. However, a well known marketing professor from a major business school who is on the firm's advisory board has certified that the firm is using a "state of the art" method that should be very accurate.

The marketing research firm has priced the report at $30,000. While the report is expensive, the president has authorized the marketing department to pay for the report from its budget if it appears that the expense is justified. If you would like to include a purchase of this new Product Positioning Report in your marketing plan, it appears on the Marketing Plan Decisions Form (Level 2) as marketing research report 7.

MARKETING PLAN DECISIONS FORM

Exhibit 5A (on page 59) is a copy of the firm's expanded Marketing Plan Decisions Form (Level 2). A concise set of instructions for completing the form begins on page 58. The blanks on the form have been filled in with the most recent decisions made by the previous marketing manager—so the form also summarizes last year's marketing plan. In the past, the marketing manager did not need to indicate the type of advertising that would be used—so that part of the form has been left blank. The form and notes are simple and clear—so they do not need further explanation here.

The president will tell you the deadline by which you will need to submit your decisions. In our firm we usually ask you to submit an electronic version of the form (which you create with the simple program described in Appendix A) as well as a paper version for verification purposes; however, in separate communication we'll update you on the details of getting the form (in paper format, computer file format, or both) to us.

FEEDBACK FOR CONTROL AND PLANNING

At the end of each year, you will receive important feedback about your plan's performance. You'll get the following reports:

1. annual financial summary,
2. a production summary,
3. the industry sales report,
4. the industry product features and prices report,
5. the industry marketing activity report, and
6. any additional marketing research reports you have purchased.

These reports should be used for control purposes—and as a basis for future planning. The format of some of these reports has recently been modified to provide the marketing department with more detailed feedback—reflecting the expanded decision areas. However, the information from the latest set of reports has been organized into the new format—so you will know what to expect. (See Exhibit 5B, starting on page 60.)

Please study these reports before developing your plan. They show the results produced by the marketing plan decisions submitted last year by the previous marketing manager (Exhibit 5A). They also summarize the firm's current financial position, your budget for the next period, and other important information.

ANNUAL FINANCIAL SUMMARY

The Financial Summary is clearly labeled and does not need much additional explanation. A few comments, however, may be helpful to you.

The unit cost, $47.00, is what it cost per unit to produce a VRD with the features specified by the previous marketing manager.

Gross sales is the revenue received from sales to dealers. You can confirm that gross sales is equal to the units sold multiplied by the wholesale price.

The cost of goods sold is computed by multiplying the number of units sold by the unit cost. (Note: some accountants refer to cost of goods sold by some other name, such as cost of sales. This firm has been using the term cost of goods sold for some time, so that term has been retained for consistency).

The gross margin is the money left after cost of goods sold is subtracted from gross sales.

The various expense items are the costs of the marketing plan submitted by the previous marketing manager. You may wish to crosscheck these expenses against the Marketing Plan Decisions Form he submitted.

Net contribution to profit (or loss) is what is left after subtracting expenses from the gross margin.

At the bottom of the financial summary is the budget that the president has set aside for the marketing department for next year. As you can see, you have up to $984,000 to spend. Based on trade association data, this amount represents about 25 percent of what all four firms in this industry will spend on marketing.

Finally, keep in mind that in this summary report each figure shown has been rounded off to a whole number. However, calculations done for the report are done before numbers are rounded off. As a result, for example, the total expenses amount shown in the report might be a dollar or two higher or lower than what you would get by adding up the rounded-off numbers.

PRODUCTION SUMMARY

The Production Summary shows requested production—the production order quantity submitted by the previous marketing manager based on his forecast of demand. Actual production was slightly higher—to meet demand for the 25,151 units actually sold. There was no excess inventory at the end of the year, so there were no transfer charges for overseas sales.

MARKETING RESEARCH REPORTS

The various marketing research reports have already been described (see Chapter 3). But Exhibit 5B provides the actual reports for this year.

Three of the marketing research reports in Exhibit 5B warrant comment. First, the firm did not purchase the Consumer Preferences Study (report number 3) last year. However, the firm has purchased it in the past—and the tables shows a range of estimates based on past reports. However, if you buy this report from the marketing research firm in the future, you will get a current report that should be more precise (within the error due to survey sampling) with estimates of average consumer preferences for different features (by segment).

Second, the Customer Shopping Habits Survey (report number 6) has never been purchased by the firm, and as a result the information found in this report is not available to the firm. However, the sample table shows the general format used in this report. If you buy this report from the marketing research firm in the future, you will get a completed report that shows the proportion of consumers from different segments who shop in each of the channels.

Third, as noted earlier, marketing research report 7 has not previously been available from the marketing research firm. However, the sample in Exhibit 5B shows its general format—based on the marketing research firm's description.

Guide to the Marketing Plan Decisions Form (Level 2)

Distribution Intensity:	The desired distribution intensity level (percent of dealers) must be specified for each channel. The minimum value is 0, implying no distribution in that channel. Otherwise, the percentage should be between the extremes of 1 percent (extremely exclusive distribution) and a maximum of 100 percent (indicating extremely intensive distribution).
Number of Sales Reps:	The number of sales representatives must be specified for each channel. Each sales rep earns $20,000 per year in salary. Each sales rep that is fired receives $5,000 in severance pay.
Percent Non-Selling Time:	This determines how much time each sales representative spends on support activities. The range is from 0 percent to 50 percent.
Sales Commission:	The minimum commission rate is 5 percent, and the maximum is 15 percent.
Customer Service:	The dollar amount that you spend on customer service must be greater than or equal to zero.
Brand name:	The brand name may be up to 10 characters long. It is used for identification on reports, and thus should not be changed once it is set in the first period.
BRAND FEATURES: --Number of special commands	The number of special commands must be between 5 and 20.
--Error Protection	The error protection rating must be between 1 and 10. A higher rating corresponds to greater error protection.
--Ease of Learning	This rating must be between 1 and 10. A higher rating corresponds to greater ease of learning.
Production Order Quantity:	The production order must be greater than or equal to 100. It should be within 20 percent of your forecast of demand for your brand to avoid inventory stock-outs if you underproduce, or to avoid transfer charges resulting from excess inventory if you overproduce.
Advertising Dollars:	Advertising spending must be greater than or equal to zero.
Type of advertising:	P=pioneering; D= direct competitive; I = indirect competitive; R= reminder; C=corporate (institutional)
Wholesale Price:	The wholesale price must be between $75 and $250; set a price for each channel. Your management will not accept a wholesale price below $75, and a wholesale price greater than $250 leads to retail prices higher than any consumers are willing to pay.

Marketing Research Reports:	You may purchase any of the following reports:	Price for Report
	1. Market Share by Segment (all brands)	$15,000
	2. Market Share by Channel (all brands)	$12,000
	3. Consumer Preference Study	$30,000
	4. Marketing Effectiveness Report	$25,000
	5. Detailed Sales Analysis (own brand)	$15,000
	6. Customer Shopping Habits Survey	$7,000
	7. Product Positioning Report	$30,000

Exhibit 5A: Marketing Plan Decision Form-Level 2

Marketing Plan Decisions - Level 2

General

Channel 1 Channel 2

30	30	Distribution intensity (% of dealers)
10	10	Number of sales reps (0-100)
10	10	Percent non-selling time (0-50%)
	5	Sales commission percent (5-15%)
$92,500		Customer service budget ($0-$9,999,999)

Marketing Research

Product 1

1. Share by segment ☑
2. Share by channel ☑
3. Preferences ☐
4. Effectiveness ☑
5. Segment by channel ☑
6. Shopping habits ☐
7. Product positioning ☐

Industry and Firm

Product 1

FirmX	Brand name (8 letters)
8	Special Commands (5-20)
3	Error Protection (1-10) (Features)
3	Ease of Learning (1-10)
25,000	Production Order Quantity (> 99)
$250,000	Advertising Spending
	Type of Advertising (P,D,I,R, or C)

Channel 1   Channel 2

| $0 | $0 | Sales Promotion |
| $95 | $95 | Wholesale Price ($75-$250) |

Note: This sample of the form is completed with the decisions made by the previous marketing manager in the last period.

Blank copies of this form appear at the end of this manual.

Exhibit 5B: Company Report for Previous Period

```
*************** Financial Summary ***************
```

FIRM X	Channel 1	Channel 2	Total
Units Sold	14074	11077	25151
Wholesale Price	$95.00	$95.00	
Unit Cost	$47.00	$47.00	
Gross Sales	$1,337,030	$1,052,315	$2,389,345
Cost of Goods Sold	$661,478	$520,619	$1,182,097
Transfer Charges			$0
Gross Margin			$1,207,248

Expenses			
Advertising			$250,000
Sales Force -Salary	$200,000	$200,000	$400,000
-Firing Costs			$0
-Commission	$66,852	$52,616	$119,468
Customer Service			$92,500
Sales Promotion	$0	$0	$0
R&D for Product Modifications			$0
Marketing Research			$67,000
Total Expenses			$928,968
Net Contribution (Loss)			$278,280

Budget for Next Period: $984,000   (25% of Industry Total)

```
*************** Production Summary ***************
```

Brand	Requested Production	Actual Production	Units Sold	Inventory Transferred	Unit Cost
FIRM X	25000	25151	25151	0	$47.

```
************** Industry Sales Report **************
```

VRD Brand	Unit Sales	Market Share (Units)	$ Sales	Market Share ($ Sales)
FIRM 1	25,151	0.250	$4,292,964	0.250
FIRM 2	25,151	0.250	$4,292,964	0.250
FIRM 3	25,151	0.250	$4,292,964	0.250
FIRM 4	25,151	0.250	$4,292,964	0.250
Total	100,604		$17,171,854	

Channel	Unit Sales	$ Sales
1	56,296	$10,696,240
2	44,308	$6,475,614

```
********** Product Features & Prices Report ***********
```

VRD Brand	Special Commands	Error Protection	Ease of Learning	Average Retail Price Channel 1	Average Retail Price Channel 2
FIRM 1	8	3	3	$190.00	$146.15
FIRM 2	8	3	3	$190.00	$146.15
FIRM 3	8	3	3	$190.00	$146.15
FIRM 4	8	3	3	$190.00	$146.15

```
*************** Marketing Activity Report ***************
            (Data Reported Is for Period 0)
```

	FIRM 1	FIRM 2	FIRM 3	FIRM 4
Advertising Dollars	$250,000	$250,000	$250,000	$250,000
Advertising Type				
Sales Promotion				
-Channel 1	$0	$0	$0	$0
-Channel 2	$0	$0	$0	$0
Number of Sales Reps				
-Channel 1	10	10	10	10
-Channel 2	10	10	10	10
Commission Rate	5%	5%	5%	5%
Customer Service	$92,500	$92,500	$92,500	$92,500

Exhibit 5B (continued)

********** Report 1: Market Share By Segment ***********

Segment Brand	Students	Home	Assistants	Creators	Managers	Parents
FIRM 1	0.250	0.250	0.250	0.250	0.250	0.250
FIRM 2	0.250	0.250	0.250	0.250	0.250	0.250
FIRM 3	0.250	0.250	0.250	0.250	0.250	0.250
FIRM 4	0.250	0.250	0.250	0.250	0.250	0.250
Total Sales (in Units)	20,028	15,084	25,104	10,240	22,056	8,092

********** Report 2: Market Share By Channel **********

Brand	Channel 1	Channel 2
FIRM 1	0.250	0.250
FIRM 2	0.250	0.250
FIRM 3	0.250	0.250
FIRM 4	0.250	0.250
Total Sales (in Units)	56,296	44,308

******* Report 3: Average Customer Preferences ********

Segment	Special Commands	Error Protection	Ease of Learning	Price Range
Students	10-13	2-4	1-3	low
Home	7-10	2-4	6-8	low
Assistants	10-13	6-8	6-8	high
Creators	12-15	2-4	4-6	high
Managers	13-16	6-8	2-4	high
Parents	5-8	2-4	7-9	low

Exhibit 5B (continued)

```
****** Report 4: Marketing Effectiveness Report ******
```

	Index	# of Competitors with Lower Index	# of Competitors with Equal or Higher Index
Awareness - FIRM X	0.550	0	3
Customer Service			
Consumer Group Rating	100%		
Industry Average Rating	100%		
Channel 1:			
Sales Rep Workload Index	100%		
Dealer Satisfaction	0.815	0	3
Channel Strength ("Push")	0.500	0	3
Channel 2			
Sales Rep Workload Index	100%		
Dealer Satisfaction	1.043	0	3
Channel Strength ("Push")	.500	0	3

```
********** Report 5: Detailed Sales Analysis **********
```

Segment	Students	Home	Assistants	Creators	Managers	Parents
FIRM X						
-Channel 1	708	936	5,080	1,578	4,752	1,020
-Channel 2	4,299	2,835	1,196	982	762	1,003

```
**********Report 6: Customer Shopping Habits[a]**********
```

Segment	Percent of Shopping in Channel 1	Percent of Shopping in Channel 2
Students	?	?
Home	?	?
Assistants	?	?
Creators	?	?
Managers	?	?
Parents	?	?

[a]Note: this report has not previously been purchased, which explains why the proportion of consumers in each segment shopping in each channel is not reported; however, the proportions would be reported if the current report is purchased.

Exhibit 5B (continued)

```
******** Report 7: Product Positioning Report
b ********
```

Brand	Students	Home	Assistants	Creators	Managers	Parents
Firm1	?	?	?	?	?	?
Firm2	?	?	?	?	?	?
Firm3	?	?	?	?	?	?
Firm4	?	?	?	?	?	?

[b]Note: this report has not previously been purchased, which explains why an estimate (index) of the "distance" of each firm's offering from each segment's ideal point is not reported; however, the question marks would be replaced with the distance numbers if the current report is purchased.

6. Supporting the Marketing Plan

Note: A staff assistant in the president's office was instructed to provide you with copies of several standard forms that have been routinely used in the company and to briefly explain the purpose of the forms. This is the set of notes prepared by the president's staff assistant.

From time to time, the president may ask you to submit a special report about your marketing strategy or other details of the marketing plan. The president will let you know if and when there is a special request. The president may also ask you to provide supporting information along with the annual Marketing Plan Decisions Form. For example, you may be asked to submit an analysis of how much profit you expect to make based on the marketing plan. To make it easier to prepare this analysis, the TMGPlan software (see Appendix A) will do the computations for you based on information you provide about your plan.

Alternatively, you can use the Marketing Budget Planning Form. A concise set of directions for completing the form appears on the next page opposite a copy of the form (Exhibit 6A); if you use the TMGPlan software, it uses the same approach described to do the calculations for you. Even if the president does not ask you to submit this information, you can use the form to evaluate the likely profitability of your plan and to compare it against the actual results you receive later in the annual financial summary.

On the back of the Marketing Budget Planning Form is a Marketing Strategy Summary Form (Exhibit 6B). You can use this form to briefly describe your planned marketing strategy and discuss the nature of competition the firm can expect to face. Again, the president may ask you to complete and submit this form. Either way, summarizing your ideas on the form can help you to keep an organized record of your strategy and give you a basis for comparing the results you actually achieve. It is also very helpful to have a written record of your strategy and how it changes over time.

Guide to the Marketing Budget Planning Form

1. Estimated Unit Sales:	Enter the expected unit sales for each channel and the total.
2. Wholesale Price:	Enter your wholesale price for each channel.
3. Unit Cost:	Compute unit cost as follows: $4 x (Number of Special Commands)+ $3 x (Error Protection Rating)+ $2 x (Ease of Learning Rating).
4. Gross Sales:	For each channel, multiply unit sales by wholesale price to determine gross sales. Add channel gross sales to get total.
5. Cost of Goods Sold:	For each channel, multiply unit sales by unit cost to determine cost of goods sold. Add channel cost of goods sold to get total.
6. Gross Margin:	Subtract total cost of goods sold from total gross sales to determine the gross margin.
7. Advertising:	Enter your advertising expenses for the period.
8. Sales Force - Salary:	Compute salary expense for each channel by multiplying the number of sales representatives by $20,000.
9. Sales Force - Firing Cost:	If the total number of sales representatives is less than last period's total, you must pay each fired sales representative $5,000 in severance pay.
10. Sales Force - Commission:	Compute commission expense for each channel by multiplying unit sales by wholesale price times commission rate.
11. Customer Service:	Enter your customer service expense for the period
12. Sales Promotion:	Enter your sales promotion expense for each channel. (optional).
13. R&D or Product Modifications:	If you have changed the features of your product, enter total product modifications expense for the period.
14. Market Research:	Enter total cost of market research reports for the period. Costs for the reports are: Report 1: $15,000 Report 2: $12,000 Report 3: $30,000 Report 4: $25,000 Report 5: $15,000 Report 6: $ 7,000 Report 7: $30,000 (optional, level 2 only)
15. Total Expenses:	Add expenses (Advertising through market research) to determine total expenses for the period.
16. Net Contribution:	Compute net profit contribution by subtracting total expenses from the gross margin.
17. Spending Against Budget:	Subtract sales force commission expense from total expenses (on line 15)

Exhibit 6A – Marketing Budget Planning Form

```
******Financial Summary / Pro Forma ******
```

Industry: ____ Firm: ____ Period: ____ Brand name: _____

	Channel 1	Channel 2	Total
(1) **Estimated Units Sold**	_____	_____	35,000
(2) **Wholesale Price**	$ 142	$ 142	
(3) **Base Unit Cost**	$ 81	$ 81	
(4) **Gross Sales** [(1) ×(2)]	$_____	$_____	$ 4,970,000
(5) **Cost of Goods Sold** [(1) × (3)]	$_____	$_____	$ 2,835,000
(6) **GROSS MARGIN** [(4) minus (5)]			$ 2,135,000
EXPENSES:			
(7) **Advertising**			$ 323,000
(8) **Sales Force-Salary**	$_____	$._____	$ 410,000
(9) **Sales Force-Firing Costs**	$_____	$_____	$_____
(10) **Sales Force-Commission**	$_____	$_____	$ 298,200
(11) **Customer Service**			$ 100,000
(12) **Sales Promotion**	$_____	$_____	$ 70,000
(13) **R&D for Product Modification**			$ 8,000
(14) **Marketing Research**			$_____
(15) **TOTAL EXPENSES** [sum of (7) to (14)]			$ 1,239,000
(16) **Net Contribution to Profit or Loss** [(6) minus (15)]			$_____
(17) **Total Spending against Budget** [(15) minus (10)]			$_____

Exhibit 6B—Marketing Strategy Summary Form

Industry: _____   Firm: _____   Period: _____

Target Market:

Product:

Place:

Promotion:

Price:

Competition:

7. A New Market Opportunity

Note: In an earlier report to the president of your firm, Market-Views, Inc.—a consulting firm—casually recommended that the firm consider adding another product. The president asked that Market-Views elaborate on the basis for that recommendation in a brief report. This is the text of Market-Views' report.

PURPOSE

Your firm currently develops and markets voice recognition devices (VRDs) for personal computers. Yet it would be short-sighted to define your market just in terms of the product you offer. Customers in the broad product-market in which you now compete have needs that are not being met by existing products. There is a possible opportunity for the firm to meet these needs and improve profits. The new opportunity might involve another target market and marketing mix in addition to the firm's current strategy. The opportunity could also take advantage of a number of the firm's strengths and resources.

The purpose of this report is to discuss this potential opportunity. First, several relevant trends in the external environment are reviewed. Next, a new product opportunity relevant to those trends is described. Then, the needs of homogeneous submarkets within the broad product-market are described. The report concludes with a brief discussion of some of the ways that product, place, promotion, and price decisions would need to be blended to develop an effective overall marketing program.

TRENDS IN THE EXTERNAL ENVIRONMENT

When personal computers first became popular, most people were only interested in running one basic application—like word processing or a spreadsheet—at a time. However, as users became more reliant on computers, they started using them in more and different ways. The new uses included personal information management (PIM) tasks—like managing address book entries, calendars, task lists, calculations, reminders, personal "alarm" messages, and email. Other more specialized uses also developed, and in most cases specially designed programs made it easy to handle the jobs that needed to be done. Improved operating systems meant that these different programs were always ready to pop-up and use—even in the middle of some other computing job. These applications became even more important in organizations where many different people needed to coordinate schedules, work, and communications.

The basic limitation in all of this was the requirement that the user be at the computer. For example, a manager might need to schedule an appointment when the computerized calendar of appointments was in another location. Customer needs for easy ways to stay "connected" prompted firms to develop and market personal digital assistants (PDAs), like those in the Palm Pilot line. As technology advanced, some of these PDAs became quite sophisticated. For example, they used built-in cell phone technologies to connect through specialized Internet service providers to websites designed to download information formatted for the tiny LCD displays of the PDAs. Designers also worked on better and easier wired and wireless ways for PDAs to connect to each other and to computer networks. So, to keep all of their information organized and up-to-date, users simply needed to keep full-featured, palm-size devices handy and ready to use.

On the other hand, keeping these devices handy and ready to use isn't always convenient. One reason is that the standard approaches for entering commands--tiny keyboards, buttons, or a stylus—are awkward. Some users have addressed this problem by using a VRD in combination with a PDA. There are several limitations with this approach, not the least of which is the requirement to carry around two different (and relatively expensive) gadgets to get some simple jobs done. Some concept testing has already shown positive consumer interest in a PDA with a built-in, purpose-specific voice recognition controller. There now appears to be even greater consumer interest in a new product concept. That concept is based on the latest generation of technology for the microchip that is at the heart of current voice recognition devices.

The Digital Vocal Communicator (DVC)—A New Concept

Several key innovations are crucial to this concept. First, some firms are successfully marketing software, including PIM applications, that run on an Internet (website) server rather than on the customer's own computer or PDA. Second, the size of the voice-recognition microchip has now been significantly reduced. Third, the producer of the microchip has developed a very inexpensive way to incorporate a simple "antenna" that serves as both a transmitter and receiver. As a result, it appears that it should be practical to develop a product that we will call a digital vocal communicator (DVC).

A DVC is small enough to be worn as a watch (yes, we realize this has a sort of Dick Tracy imagery) or as a lapel pin. As with a standard VRD, it would interpret spoken language commands. One thing that makes it possible to keep the DVC so small is that all processing would be done by streaming digital signals to and from software that runs on the VRD firm's Internet server. This would happen without a dedicated Internet connection because each DVC's antenna would help to relay signals to and from the Internet server. While this concept would not work in isolated wilderness areas, it would work well in populated urban areas. It would connect even better over time as more devices were put in service because there would be more "relay points" in the network of antennas.

A DVC wouldn't be useful for complicated computer tasks that require the user to be able to see or hear extensive computer output. But it would work for many of the personal information management jobs (including email) that are handled with PDA applications. The user would use voice commands to control the various applications (and to dictate messages that would be stored in digital form). While feedback from the computer to the user would be limited, it would be in the form of spoken/audio output from a tiny speaker in the device. The customer's data would be "passed through" the website so it could be synchronized on the customer's desktop computer. In combination, it appears that the digital vocal communicator (DVC) will work very well for a variety of standard PDA/PIM type applications.

No one else has yet developed a practical DVC. However, your license agreements with the maker of the microchip give you a special opportunity to take advantage of these developments. Expertise you have already developed in creating instruction sets for the VRD could be directly applicable to developing voice commands for personal information management applications to run from the web server. Finally, because of your close working relationship and license agreement with the microchip producer, you will be able to get needed technical information in advance.

Of course, your three current rivals have a similar relationship with the microchip producer. One or more of them might already be pursuing this idea. It is difficult to predict which might enter the market, or when. And the license agreement with the microchip producer sets standards that ensure that basic commands for your DVC also work with a DVC produced by one of these other firms.

A few examples will help to give you an idea of how a customer might use a DVC (and the web-server applications to which it communicates).

► a student rushing to class speaks into the DVC, instructs it to open a new email message, dictates a brief message to a friend about getting together for lunch, and sends the message;

► a manager who is in a taxi after a visit with an out-of-town client uses the DVC to confirm the departure time for her flight home, and to set a reminder to check back with the client by phone the following week;

► a busy mom driving home from work updates her "to do" list and then downloads and listens to a brief audio message from her kids;

► a newspaper reporter who is doing research interviews at a trade show dictates a first draft of his story and sends it to the business editor for a quick reaction.

► on the way to lunch, an administrative assistant sees his boss who asks for a copy of a spreadsheet file; while waiting in line to get a sandwich, the assistant speaks into the DVC and sends a file transfer command over the Internet to copy the file from his network folder to his boss's network folder.

PRODUCT-MARKET SEGMENTS

As the examples above indicate, the characteristics and needs of the people in the broad product-market in this area are quite heterogeneous. Different people have different reasons for wanting a DVC and they will use it in different ways. But there are more homogeneous market segments within the broad product-market. In fact, the people who are aggregated into distinct segments with respect to voice recognition device needs also tend to share common preferences for DVCs. The general characteristics of these segments have been described in an earlier report. Here, the focus is on the benefits they tend to seek from a DVC and the associated web-server applications.

The Modern Students

Students are always on the go, are used to communicating with friends and teachers by computer, and like the idea of being spontaneous, yet connected. As a result, they are excited about the DVC concept and think that being able to use a few basic DVC applications in standard ways would be very convenient. On the other hand, they have less interest in the variety of possible information management applications and see them as less essential to getting their assignments done. Consistent with that and their budget limits, they tend to be the most price sensitive segment. Since students do not anticipate using a lot of different DVC applications, they'd prefer to keep the commands for the applications they do use simple.

The Home Users

The people in this segment also like the DVC concept, but they tend to be less motivated than students to try the idea. They are also different in that they want a variety of different DVC applications. One important reason is that more than one member of a family might use the DVC. In addition, different members might use different DVC capabilities for different tasks. A busy Little League coach, for example, might use the DVC to schedule batting practice for different kids on the team. A busy mom might want to quickly record ideas for a new spaghetti sauce recipe … while checking cookbooks at a local bookstore. A teenager might just want to send a previously prepared digital birthday card to a friend as an email attachment. The home users like the flexibility of a DVC that can perform a number of different special-purpose tasks. But not everyone bothers to learn all of the possibilities. Rather, each person focuses on what they need most often. In short, many people in this segment see a DVC as a good way to gain more effective use of their spare time. They say that a moderate price would make the purchase easier and allow different family members to enjoy the flexible benefits.

The Harried Assistants

The harried administrative assistants often must deal with a wide host of DVC applications and they're always being pulled away from their desktop computers. They see a DVC as a way to be better organized and not let some of their job responsibilities "fall between the cracks." Thus, the DVC concept has significant potential with this segment. But, at the same time, many firms have found that these employees feel overwhelmed when they have to learn more and more technologies to do the same job in different ways. On the other hand, company specialists can help setup the DVC for an assistant's specific needs and help with training. The trick is to achieve a balance between getting the most useful combination of DVC tasks and ease of use. Many firms think that if this balance can be achieved, the DVC will pay for itself quickly. It helps the assistant save time, be better organized, and get more work done.

The Professional Creators

These people were often innovators and excited about using the original VRDs, but fewer of them are certain that the DVC will closely fit their needs and requirements. For one thing, they tend to spend more time working in front of a computer, so many of them doubt that the wireless communication benefits of the DVC would prove to be that useful. On the other hand, they do tend to work independently, at least compared to people in most other jobs. As a result, they usually handle their own appointments, communications, calendars, address books, messages and a host of other personal information management needs. Because of this, being able to perform a very wide array of tasks with a DVC is appealing. They also don't seem to be put off by the technical details of learning what DVC command is required to do what job. Perhaps this just reflects their confidence in using computers to setup software that matches their personal preferences for how to work. Those professional creators who think that the DVC might save time see it as a good business investment.

The High-Tech Managers

The high-tech managers like the DVC idea, and because they tend to be out of the office more it is probably more useful for them than for some other people, like the professional creators. On the other hand, managers who say that they would probably buy a DVC seem to be mainly interested in a limited set of possible applications; they note that they have good support back in the office for most of the routine work. Even though the company would pay for the DVC, these managers seem more sensitive about the price point for DVCs than VRDs, perhaps because they don't want to look foolish by spending a lot of money for something that may not prove to be that critical to what they do.

The Concerned Parents

Most members of this segment are not really in the market. They want their kids to have a good experience with technology and computers—and a VRD helps to accomplish that objective. But many of them believe that a DVC isn't really meant for kids. The parents in this segment who express interest in DVCs seem to want a very simple product—one that just introduces the child to the idea. In general, they think that there are better ways to spend money on their kids.

MARKET POTENTIAL

Clearly, the broad product-market for DVCs is still in the introductory part of the product life cycle. However, based on the earlier success of personal digital assistants, experts think that the market will quickly move into the early growth stage once DVCs are introduced, especially if they are well tuned to market needs and if there is enough industry promotional effort to spark interest. On the other hand, our forecasts suggest that the overall demand for DVCs will not be as large as the demand for VRDs. While it is difficult to develop a precise forecast for such a new product, we believe that initial DVC sales potential is perhaps only about half what it is for voice recognition devices. But demand is expected to continue to grow for a number of years—especially if product refinements fit customer expectations and needs. In combination, this suggests that there should be profitable opportunities now and in the future.

The market potential for DVCs is likely to depend on the same factors as the market potential for VRDs. Specifically, these factors include the size of the different segments, growth trends, how well the marketing mixes meet customers' needs, and the extent to which potential customers are aware of the DVC concept and what it can do for them.

Your firm's previous experience with the segments in this market should give you some initial ideas about their computer usage and their consumer behavior. However, keep in mind that the growth trends for a new and different product may be quite different. Further, the target market that appears to offer your firm the best opportunities for VRDs may not be the best target market for DVCs.

Industry experts agree that the overall level of industry advertising will affect market growth. Most customers are completely unfamiliar with DVC ideas, and it requires some new ways of thinking about information. However, familiarity (and demand) are likely to increase if your firm—and competitors—spend money on pioneering advertising that helps to inform customers about the product class. The product life cycle for this product may even move rapidly, especially if the quality of communicator(s) is good. But if a number of firms enter the market, advertising with a competitive thrust will quickly replace pioneering efforts.

As always, growth in the broad product-market—or in segments of the market—will depend on how successfully marketing mixes meet customers' needs. Some customers may be willing to buy a DVC that is not exactly what they want—and will select the one that comes closest to their ideal. On the other hand, many potential customers will just wait—and not buy anything until the right product is available in the right place at the right price. Further, different segments have different needs. Thus, different marketing strategies—different marketing mixes for different target markets—may be required.

This last point is an important one—so it is useful to consider several strategy decision areas within the 4Ps.

DEVELOPING THE MARKETING MIX

Product

There can be many technical differences in how the DVC concept is implemented. But research shows that most customers are likely to simplify their evaluation process by grouping features into three main areas: (1) the number and variety of tasks (specialized server-based applications controlled by the DVC), (2) how similar the voice commands are for different applications, and (3) the extent to which the specific applications can be customized by the user. Different customers seem to have quite different needs and interests with respect to these features, so it is useful to discuss them in more detail.

▶ *Number of Tasks*

All DVCs will ultimately support one or two basic personal information management tasks—like sending/receiving brief email messages and controlling an address book function. At the other extreme, a DVC is less well suited for applications that require the user to be able to see or hear extensive computer output. Developing these more complex applications to run on a web server would also put the firm in direct competition with well-established software firms. On the other hand, it is possible to produce a DVC and more focused server-based applications that handle 9 or 10 different, and commonly used, personal information management tasks. For example, it is possible to build DVC programs that allow the user to manage an appointments calendar, reminder functions, a notepad capability, and a task manager—all with vocal commands and away from standard computer support. There are many other possibilities. But the total number of tasks is limited to 9 or 10.

While it can be convenient to have the capability to handle a number of different tasks at the same time, not all customers want or need the variety. For example, it doesn't help to have a DVC that can handle an appointments calendar if the user doesn't keep a detailed calendar, or conversely if someone else is making most of the appointments. In addition, creating the capability for a DVC to handle a larger number of tasks is more costly (for the firm and for customers) and slows down the processing of vocal commands.

There is another drawback. The likelihood of a problem or unintended side effect increases with the number of tasks added. For example, a task manager that plays audio reminder messages at scheduled times might work fine in combination with some other tasks, but not all. If the user is trying to send an email message at the same time reminder messages are scheduled to play, problems may occur. In such a case, the DVC might even "drop" communications and lose some of the information. Computer magazines and dealers will probably warn novice users to avoid such hassles—and stick to the basic combinations. Novice users may do just that. But, some confident computer users who love the ability to handle as many tasks as possible will want much more than the basic combinations.

► *Similarity of Commands*

Since individual applications for different DVC tasks do quite specific things, they each contain only a few commands that are easy to learn. But there's a potential drawback here too. Since each application must have its own set of commands, the software may be designed so that some of the same commands are used in different applications. Conversely, each application may have its own unique commands. What's good is not always clear. It depends on the preferences of the user.

Having very similar commands across different tasks makes them easier to use. But keeping everything consistent can be awkward when the tasks are different. For example, a certain vocal command might be used to set the time in an alarm clock program. The designer might try to use that same command in a similar way in an address book program. This sounds reasonable, but what is the equivalent of setting the time in an address book? Is it selecting the telephone number, or is it setting the zip code for the mailing area? As you can see from this example, the idea of having similar commands for slightly different tasks may make operation more difficult. Still, people who use a DVC less frequently prefer that the commands be similar across programs. Contrastly, people who use a DVC a lot prefer that commands be different for different tasks. Their higher usage enables them to learn the commands quickly.

► *Ability to Customize*

DVC applications are designed to handle basic tasks, but that doesn't mean that all users have the same preferences for how things work. For example, a busy executive might want a task manager that will list "to-do" items by importance while a student might want his "to-do" list organized by due date. The ability to customize to these different personal preferences is standard in most "desktop" PIM software packages. However, adding this ability to DVC applications that rely on vocal commands is harder. Sometimes there is a conflict between the commands for a primary DVC task and the customizing options for another task. For example, a verbal command that deletes an email message may use the same language as a command in a reminder program that automatically deletes reminder messages after they are sent. After all, there are only so many combinations of commands that make sense.

This problem can be reduced by allowing the user to modify the server-based applications with a personalized setup. This makes it possible to customize the choice of commands used for both primary tasks and option settings.

But this customizing requires that the customer do more work initially and understand more technical details. It's time-consuming—and it's easy to make errors. The DVC company can provide detailed instructions that help to prevent problems—but the customer must still wade through all the technical detail and spend the time to get everything right.

Of course, customizing flexibility is not an all-or-nothing feature. The real question is how much of this capability to build into the software. For example, at a simple level the customizing might allow a user to just indicate the volume sensitivity of a DVC's microphone. At a more advanced level, the user might be able to customize 9 or 10 features. Remember that the greater the ability to customize the greater the cost of developing the software and the greater the retail price to the customer. Certainly some users will pay more if they can customize the DVC applications to their specific preferences. In short, the decision must be based on the needs and preferences of a specific target market.

▶ *Product Modifications*

DVC capability depends on the hardware and the server-based applications. Thus, future upgrades will require that applications be modified and updated. In addition, consumers' preferences for different types of applications may change, so DVCs may need to be updated regularly. The annual computer trade show forces a schedule on this work. New products must be ready in time for demonstrations at the trade show. If you introduce a DVC, you will need to do it at the same time you release a modified version of your VRD.

Keep in mind that this could prove to be a very competitive market. If other firms are developing their own versions of a DVC, they are keeping it a secret. Similarly, it would be wise for you to wait and announce your plans to the industry only after it is too late for a competitor to adjust for your actions. On the other hand, figuring out the right speed to market is a complex decision. There may be an advantage in being an early entrant with a new offering. On the other hand, there is certainly the risk of making costly mistakes if you move too quickly. So, it may make sense to get more specific market research information about this market before proceeding.

▶ *Product Costs*

Based on data from your firm's accounting and R&D departments, it's possible to estimate several key costs relevant to the new product. These should be considered in any decision to introduce the new product and—if the product is introduced—in the annual marketing plan.

The initial cost to develop the new product and the software—and the cost of any subsequent modifications—depends on the levels selected for the three product features. This approach is summarized below.

▶ R&D Product Modification Costs for the DVC

FEATURE	FEASIBLE RANGE	Cost to Change Level from Previous Period	
		To Decrease Level	*To Increase Level*
Number of tasks	1-10	no cost	$8,000×(change)×(change)
Similarity of commands	1-10	no cost	$5,000×(change)×(change)
Ability to customize	1-10	$3,000×(change)	$3,000×(change)×(change)

In this table, change refers to the difference in the level of the feature from one period to the next. The very first time the product is offered, the level of the feature is the amount of change—since the features would in effect start at the level 0. Total product modification (or product development) cost is the sum of the costs to change individual features.

These cost considerations suggest that it will be quite expensive to develop an initial model of the product, especially if higher levels on features seem appropriate. In that case, it might be worth evaluating the idea of developing a prototype that is less rich in features as a step toward a final design.

The level of the different product features will also directly affect the unit production cost (which includes the cost of both the hardware and the server-based applications). Specifically,

Unit production cost = $4 × (Number of tasks) +

$3 × (Similarity of commands) +

$2 × (Ability to customize).

Thus, the unit cost for a DVC might vary from $9 to $90 depending on the features of the product.

Place

The new software could be distributed to the target market through the firm's existing channels of distribution. However, you may need to rethink your Place strategy. Experience in the VRD market indicates that different segments tend to prefer different channels. If the target market for your new marketing mix shops in a channel that you haven't emphasized in the past, you may need to recruit more or different middlemen.

On the other hand, it makes sense to blend your different strategies so that you take advantage of the channel relationships you have or can develop. Specifically, you may improve your competitive position if you go after a target market that shops in a channel in which you already have a strong presence.

Further, you need to keep in mind that your channel focus will affect promotion decisions as well.

Promotion

Basically, you will face the same opportunities and limitations in promoting both the DVC and VRD products. Thus, we will review issues in this area only briefly.

▶ *Personal Selling*

Having a second product could result in some economies of scale in personal selling. Sales reps spend lots of time traveling, planning, and doing other non-selling-related activities. But, once a rep is with the customer, it would not take long to discuss a second product. Of course, each rep could not cover as many accounts if there were more work to do at each account. But it is clear that adding a second product would not require doubling the size of the sales force.

How much additional selling effort might be required would depend on how selling effort is currently allocated between the two channels. If your new target market requires increased distribution intensity in one channel or the other, you may need to add new sales reps. Moreover, the type of channel that a rep calls on will influence how effort is split between selling and supporting activities.

Making these decisions wisely for two products—not just one—will be a bit more challenging. But the challenge is not so great that the opportunity should be screened out on this basis alone.

▶ *Advertising*

Advertising is another area where there might be efficiency in having two products. Your firm could advertise more than one product in an ad and on its website—and customer familiarity with one of your brands will probably have a positive spillover effect on the other. Of course, no advertising decision is ever simple. The advertising objectives for the new marketing mix or target market may be different than at present. And, advertising adjustments may be needed if the nature of competition is different for the two products.

▶ *Sales Promotion*

Sales promotion can be used in basically the same way for the DVC and your original voice recognition device. However, sales promotion objectives and tools may need to be adjusted to accommodate a broader product line, a different target market, a different channel, and the rest of the promotion blend.

Price

Computer industry experts are predicting that retail prices for DVCs will range from about $60 to $250—depending on the features, the manufacturer, and the channel(s) in which it is distributed. This is a broad price range, but marketing research surveys suggest that there is also a broad range in the reference prices that different types of consumers give when asked how much they would pay for a DVC.

A wholesale price would need to be set taking into consideration costs, how channel markups will influence the final price, and how your target market would respond to that price. However, your DVC does not have to be priced at the same level of your voice recognition device. To the contrary, in other computer-related product-markets, consumers have come to expect that firms may offer one product, say a personal digital assistant, at a high price but another product, like a network interface card, at a low price.

Dealers who sell DVCs can be expected to stick to their customary markup percent. So traditional dealers in Channel 1 would use a 50 percent markup for the DVC, and the limited-service Internet sellers in Channel 2 would apply a 35 percent markup.

CUSTOMER CHOICES AMONG BRANDS

It's difficult to predict exactly how potential customers might react to one brand or another. But most customers will view this as an important decision. Thus, they will look for a product with features that meet their needs—at the right price.

Having the new product in the right place will certainly make a difference. Customers tend to shop for new computer products where they've purchased before—and, in some cases, the dealer's sales rep can significantly influence the decision.

The possibility of a customer who already owns a VRD buying a DVC from the same producer warrants special consideration. Certainly, brand awareness can make a difference when different brands are close substitutes. But experience in other computer-related markets suggests that customers are not very loyal to a particular producer, especially when the two products are not highly interdependent. Rather, customers evaluate different products separately—and don't hesitate to buy from different producers. This can be good or bad—depending on your viewpoint. It means that you don't need to focus on the same target market for the two different products. On the other hand, it also means that your current strengths with a particular target market may not transfer to the new marketing mix.

MARKETING RESEARCH

Marketing research can help provide information about this new market opportunity. Your firm's marketing information system (MIS) and staff could certainly keep you informed of general developments in the DVC market, just as they do for the established voice recognition device market. In particular, the reports on industry sales, product features and prices, and marketing activity that you routinely receive should be updated to include information on different DVC brands as they are introduced in the market.

In addition, the same outside research firm that provides the studies of the voice recognition device has announced that it will also offer similar reports on the DVC market. However, it does not see a need to prepare a new version of report 6—Customer Shopping Habits Survey—because there is no reason to expect shopping habits to differ for the new product. Costs for the DVC reports will generally be the same as they are for the VRD. The exception is the Marketing Effectiveness Report (report 4). It will continue to cost $25,000 if ordered for one product—whether VRD or DVC; however, if it is ordered for both products the combined cost will be only $30,000.

CONCLUSION

This report reviews a possible opportunity in the broad product-market in which you compete. It explains the changes that have led to that opportunity, provides some information about the needs of different segments of the broad market, and raises issues relevant to marketing mix planning.

Keep in mind, however, that important resource considerations are also relevant. Resources would be required to develop a successful product—and any additional marketing expenses would need to be considered relative to your firm's marketing budget. In other words, this is a decision that may require top management approval. If approval is given, top management will need to determine if additional resources, perhaps in the form of a discretionary budget, can be made available to the marketing department.

We have briefly reviewed the firm's internal planning procedures and related software. It appears that adding a second product would only require minor changes in the firm's Marketing Plan Decisions Form. We have provided a sample of our recommendation for an advanced form (Level 3) on the next page. It appears there is a good opportunity here for growth in sales and profits. However, there are also risks and some complications. Competitors' reactions and plans could be very important.

We hope that this report provides a good base from which you can decide whether to pursue this opportunity—or instead devote your resources to doing an even better job with your current markets.

Exhibit 7A: Marketing Plan Decisions Form-Level 3

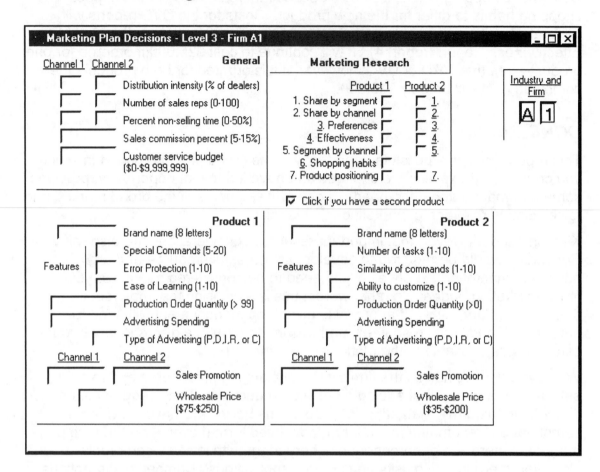

Note: On this form, if you have a second product, there should be a check mark beside the "click if you have a second product", and all of the decisions for Product 2 should be completed. If you don't have a second product, there should not be a check, and the Product 2 decisions should not be completed (and if any of those decisions were filled in they would be ignored).

Blank copies of this form appear at the end of this manual.

Appendix A. Marketing Plan Software

Note: This appendix is a set of instructions prepared by the company's IT department on how to use the TMGPlan software. The president may indicate that you are not required to use the program. However, if you do use it this material overviews some of the information that is available in the program's online help system. From the outset, keep in mind that the program uses a PASSWORD to limit access to information. The firm is very concerned about security of confidential information; you must keep track of your password or you may lose your job! At the end of the appendix there is also a brief discussion of the TMGftp program, which the firm is thinking of using so managers can submit their Plan files over the Internet.

Introduction

The information technology department has developed a Windows program, called TMGPlan, that can help the marketing department do its job.

At a basic level, TMGPlan provides an electronic version of the Marketing Plan Decisions Form and allows you to easily create a password-protected computer file with the values for your new marketing plan. If you wish, you can open and view a previously-created Plan file, modify the decision values, and save it again.

The software can also help you evaluate your plan (or a preliminary version of it) by computing and displaying the Pro Forma Financial Summary that shows the revenue and costs (as well as profit or loss) that your plan will produce if your sales forecast is accurate (for example, if you sell all of what you produce). It also computes the total expense of the plan that will be charged against the marketing department budget.

The Plan file created by the program is in a special format that is ready to be submitted to the president. Because of the need to prevent unauthorized people from having access to our propriety company information, the file is password protected.

The program also allows you to open a previously-created Plan file and view its contents, modify it, and save it again. In order to do this, you must know the password that was used when the Plan file was originally saved. (Plan files are stored in a special format that is understood only by TMGPlan and software used by the president's staff; Plan files cannot be viewed with a word processor or any other program).

TMGPlan also has a file viewer that makes it easy for you to browse through (and print, if you have a printer) reports that are provided to you by the president or his staff. However, the IT department is concerned that "hackers" may gain access to confidential company data. As a result, IT is considering a recommendation that reports be provided to you only in password-protected format. In that event, **you will not be able to access, view, or print the contents of the report unless you know the exact password that was used to submit the marketing plan for that period.**

It is a matter of extreme importance to the company, and to you, that you keep a confidential record of the password you use to submit reports. It is highly recommended that you use the same password in each plan period so as to avoid confusion, especially if several marketing managers are working together in a team effort and will need access to the information!

The president may decide that it is sufficient for you to submit a printed copy of the Marketing Plan Decisions Form without an electronic file. It is also possible to use the Marketing Budget Planning Form in Chapter 6—instead of the software—to prepare a pro forma. Thus, you may not need to use this software. But it is here if you want or need it

---

▶ *Some Key Points About Using the TMGPlan Software*

- A password system limits access to proprietary information.

- Creates a computer file named Plan*id*.TMG (where 'id' is replaced with the letter for the firm's TMG Industry and the firm's number) that is an electronic version of the Marketing Plan Decisions Form to submit to the president.

- Has a complete online help system; access it by pressing the F1 key or by selecting the Help button.

- Does calculations on financial and budget implications of a plan.

- Opens and displays password-protected reports.

- Prints (completed) decision forms and reports.

Installing the TMGPlan Program and Help File

System Requirements

The TMGPlan software is designed for use on computers that use Microsoft Windows 95, 98, 2000, Me, or NT. (You may be able to use the software on a computer that runs Windows 3.1. Please see the notes in the readme.txt file on the CD for details).

To install the software distributed with the manual you need a CD drive. However, if your computer does not have a CD drive you can transfer the program to floppy disks by using a computer that does have a CD drive; see the readme.txt file on the CD-Rom for details.

To install the software you need about 3 megabytes of free space on your hard drive. To use the software the computer must have at least 16 megabytes of available memory (RAM). You will also need a mouse or other pointing device in addition to a keyboard. The program uses about 3 megabytes of memory when it is running. If you don't have much memory, close other programs before you start TMGPlan.

Printing features of the program are disabled if it is run on a computer that does not have a printer (or if the Windows printer driver for the printer is not properly installed).

The separate tutorial program requires a multimedia PC with a sound card and speakers.

Installation Procedure

Insert the CD-Rom in the computer's CD drive (and if necessary close the drive door). Watch to see if there is an indication (flashing light, sound, etc.) that the CD reader is active. In most cases, the installation procedure will start automatically. Then, simply follow the instructions that appear on the screen. If the installation procedure does not start automatically when you insert the CD in the drive, click Start, and then Run, and then click browse to select the Setup.exe file on the CD, and then click OK.

Please be certain to read the license agreement before you install the software. If you do not wish to agree to the terms of the license agreement you can cancel the installation procedure.

The standard installation installs the program (TMGPlan.exe), help file (TMGPlan.hlp). and the tutorial (TMGTutor.exe) as a subfolder of the Windows programs files folder. The standard path is:
c:\program files\tmg\tmgplan\

You may change this default folder and install the software in another folder, but if so you will need to remember where you installed it to be able to start and run the program.

When you install the software, it is a good idea to check the Readme.txt file. It may include information that became available after these printed materials were produced.

Using the TMGPlan Program

How to Start the Program (and Exit from It)

To start the software, click on the Start button, click on Programs, click on TMG, and then click on the TMGPlan icon in the Program Files list. A title screen will briefly appear and then the main Setup and Selection Screen appears. At this point, you enter values and select what you want to do. [Note, you can create a "shortcut" icon to start the program from the Windows desktop by first right clicking on the icon on the Start programs file list and then click Send to>Windows desktop(create shortcut)].

The program is very easy to use and works like other standard Windows programs. In addition, explanations ("hints" on what to do next) appear in the status bar at the bottom of the screens as you move the cursor over various data entry boxes, or you can use the Tab key to "highlight" any of the buttons. Then, by simply pressing the F1 key, you get context-sensitive help related to the highlighted item. Alternatively, you can access help by clicking the Help button that is on each major screen or by clicking the Help item on the menu at the top of the screen. If you have never used a Windows program or are unfamiliar with how help works, click on the Help menu bar item at the top of the program, and then in the drop-down list that appears click the Help on Help entry.

When you are finished working with TMGPlan, press the Exit button, which appears on every major screen. On screens with drop-down menus, you may also select the Exit menu item from the File menu. When you ask to exit the program, a confirmation box will appear, asking you to verify that you want to exit. Any marketing plan information you may have entered but not yet saved will be lost if you exit the program.

If you encounter any problems installing or using the software you should check the website for troubleshooting tips.

It's probably easiest to just give the program a try; messages will let you know if you do something wrong—and experimenting can't hurt anything. Once you've reviewed the "The Crucial Things You Should Know from the Start" section below and tried the software you'll see that you don't need to worry much about memorizing directions here. It's all straight forward and the help system provides online advice about any questions you may have.

Crucial Things You Should Know from the Start

There's a Complete Online Help System

The TMGPlan program features a complete online help system. If you have used help with any other Windows program, this one works the same way. To get help at any point in the program, press the F1 key or select the Help button on the screen.

To exit from help and return to the TMGPlan program, you can press the esc key, click the Exit button that is on the button bar at the top of the help window, or click the small x in the upper right hand corner of the help window.

There is a status bar at the bottom of the screen that provides hints about what to do. As you move the mouse and the cursor moves over the over different parts of the screen, the hint will change to be specific to that part of the screen.

Level and Firm Identification Information

When you start the program you need to know your firm identification (id) code. The firm id code consists of the letter for your industry and the number for your firm (as provided by the president). For example, if you are firm 3 in industry B, your firm id code is B3.

You also need to know the (game) level for the plan form you will be using. The level value is 1, 2, or 3 as per instructions from the president's office. Level 1 applies to standard marketing department responsibilities (as described in Chapter 4 of this manual). Level 2 applies to expanded marketing department responsibilities (as described in Chapter 5). And Level 3 applies if the president authorizes introduction of a new product (Chapter 7).

The Password

When you save a plan with the TMGPlan program, you specify a password. The president will tell you what password to use (or, may tell you that you can select a password on your own). It is important to keep track of this password, as is explained in more detail below.

Understanding the Names of Files Used by TMGPlan

TMGPlan uses special file names. These names are important to the smooth operation of TMGPlan (and the overall game). Do not rename these files. If you do, neither your software nor the president's software will be able to locate or read the files.

File names are based on a simple combination of information:

- the content of the file (plan, pro forma statement, or report),
- your firm's id code (industry identification letter and firm number), and
- the file type (a password-protected TMG file or a regular text (TXT) file.

For example, a Plan file for firm 3 in industry A is called PLANA3.TMG. A password-protected Report file for that firm is called REPORTA3.TMG, and the unencrypted (standard text) file version of the report would be REPORTA3.TXT.

Once a Plan file has been saved with a particular password, no one (including you) except the president can open, view, or modify that file without knowing that exact password. Similarly, no one will be able to view, print, or unencrypt a REPORTid.TMG file unless they can provide the password used when the plan for that period was saved. So, you need to remember your password! (For more information about the password system, check the topic File Security, Passwords, and Encryption in the online help).

The file names do not change from one plan period to the next and are the same regardless of what level of plan is involved.

It is the PLANid.TMG decision file that you submit to the president. The PROFRMid.TXT and REPORTid.TMG (or REPORTid.TXT) files are for your use.

Saving a Plan File Overwrites Previously Created File

It is very important to understand that each time you save a Plan file, the TMGPlan program overwrites any previously saved Plan file that is in the default folder and replaces it with a file that is based on the values currently shown on the Marketing Plan Decisions Form screen.

On the other hand, if you try unsuccessfully to save a plan (for example, if you see a message that says you need to finish entering or correcting values before the plan can be saved), then a Plan file that already exists in the default folder is not overwritten.

If you want to save the final version of a Plan file for future reference, you may want to copy it to a folder different from the default folder before you create and save a new plan (which would otherwise overwrite the old one).

TMGPlan Program Messages

The TMGPlan program sends you different messages (confirmation, information, warning, or error). Messages appear in small windows. The window indicates the type of message and each message box has one or more buttons. You will need to click a button to continue. The buttons vary depending on the nature of the message; however, warning and error message windows, and some informational message boxes include a Help button. If you click this Help button, you will receive more detailed information on the message and the situation, which will guide you in deciding what to do next.

Overview of Different TMGPlan Screens

The TMGPlan program displays a series of screens (windows) to help you with different tasks. On most screens there are several basic types of controls, including:

A status (hints) bar at the bottom of the screen: this provides information about the screen you are viewing. The bar is updated as you move the cursor to different parts of the screen.

Edit fields: these are small boxes (in which you type setup or decision values). A label beside each box describes what you need to type. If you put the cursor over a box, additional information will be displayed in the status bar at the bottom of the screen;

Buttons: these are rectangular boxes with labels that you click to select a particular action. For example, most screens feature an Exit button, a Help button, and other buttons specific to where you are in the program;

A menu bar: A menu bar may appear at the top of the screen offering choices such a File, Help, etc. If you click a menu selection, a drop-down menu appears that gives you additional choices. For the most part, the menus just give you another way to do what you can do more directly by clicking a button. However, some less frequently accessed options are available only as menu selections. For example, the File menu on the initial screen gives you a way to select the Windows printer that TMGPlan will use for printing, and the Help menu gives you a selection of help alternatives.

The screen names and what they do are summarized in the next section.

Screen Names and Brief Description

▶ Setup and Selection Screen

This is the main screen, where you specify required setup information such as industry letter code, firm number, game level, and the directory in which you want TMGPlan to save and locate files. The screen also contains buttons that allow you to select other functions.

▶ Marketing Plan Decisions Screen

This screen allows you to create or modify the Plan file containing all individual decisions for your firm's marketing plan for this decision period. From this point you can save the Plan file (with a password that you enter), print a copy of the completed Plan form, or evaluate a pro forma.

▶ Inputs for Pro Forma Screen

This screen collects information that is not included in your current marketing plan but that is necessary to compute the Pro Forma Financial Summary.

▶ Pro Forma Financial Estimates Screen

This screen displays new financial estimates (based on your inputs to the previous screen) and, if you wish, prints and/or saves them to a file.

▶ File Viewer Screen

The File Viewer Screen allows you to decrypt, view, print, and save Report files. You can also use it to open a previously saved Pro Forma file.

▶ Password Entry Window

This window accepts the password used for encryption of Plan and Report files.

The sections below provide more information about the major screens. *For more detail on any issue, check the online Help.*

Setup and Selection Screen

The Setup and Selection Screen is the starting place for using TMGPlan. The first thing you need to do is enter the required setup information, which consists of a letter (A-Z) identifying your industry, your firm number (1-4), and the level of the Marketing Game (1, 2, or 3). The president will provide you with this information. Next, you need to select the default folder for files (discussed below). You must complete this setup before you can do anything else (for example, create a new plan, modify an existing plan, or review a report).

Default Folder for Files

This area of the Setup and Selection Screen allows you to specify the drive and folder that you would like to use as the default location for files used by TMGPlan.

To change the drive letter, click on the arrow next to the current drive letter. A list of available drives will drop down. Click on (highlight) the drive you want to use. If you are selecting a drive with removable disks (floppy disk drive, ZIP drive), insert a disk in the drive before selecting it. (If the drive is empty when you select it, you may receive the message "I/O error 21"; if this happens, click "OK" in the message window, insert a disk in the drive, and select the drive again).

After you have set the correct drive, a list of folders available on that drive will appear in the Folders box. Use the scroll bar to scroll through the list. Double-click on a folder to show subfolders below it, or to select it as the default.

After you have set the correct drive and folder, the List of Files box will show a list of files in the selected folder. You can use the scroll bars to scroll through the list. (You do not need to select a file from the list; rather, this is just a way to verify what files are already in the folder).

Use Values as Default Check Box

This check box controls whether or not the setup values you specify will be saved for reuse the next time you start the program. If the box is checked, the values will be saved when you exit TMGPlan and show the next time you start the program. If the box is not checked, the current values are not saved as the defaults.

If you are using TMGPlan on a computer in a computer lab or in another "shared" setting, it is best to leave this box unchecked; otherwise, your values will appear as the default when the next user starts the program.

Selection Buttons for Setup and Selection Screen

The following selection buttons are available on the Setup and Selection Screen. You click a button to pick the next thing you want to do. The purpose of the buttons are briefly described below.

▶ *Prepare New Marketing Plan Button*

Click this button to go to the Marketing Plan Decisions Screen and enter a new marketing plan. You must enter valid setup information before selecting this button.

▶ *Open/Modify Existing Plan Button*

Click this button to go to the Marketing Plan Decisions Screen and review or modify an existing marketing plan. You must enter valid setup information before selecting this button. In addition, a Plan file for your firm must exist in the default folder you specified. In order to open it, you will need to provide the password with which this file was originally saved.

▶ *Review or Print a Report Button*

Click this button to go to the File Viewer Screen. You must enter valid setup information before selecting this button. Once there, you will be able to select a directory in which to search for a file; in other words, the file you wish to view or print does not have to be in your default folder. However, if the file is password protected (that is, has the TMG file extension), you will need to know the password to be able to open it. Once you have opened a file, this screen also allows you to print files, save them under other names, and search through them to find specific words or phrases.

▶ *Help Button*

Click this button to get help on the Setup and Selection Screen, or for that matter on other aspects of TMGPlan.

▶ *Exit Button*

Click this button to exit TMGPlan. If you selected the Use Values as Defaults check box, your default setup information will be saved before you exit.

Menus for Setup and Selection Screen

A menu bar with several menu choices appears at the top of the Setup and Selection Screen. For the most part, menu items just give you another way to do things that you can do more simply by clicking one of the buttons on the screen. However, the menus do give you access to a few capabilities that you are not likely to need frequently. For example, under the File menu there is an option to choose which printer you want to use. Similarly, the Help menu gives you a variety of help-related choices, including a selection for getting help on using the help system.

Marketing Plan Decisions Screen

The Marketing Plan Decisions Screen displays edit boxes to allow you to enter and view values for all of the decisions in your marketing plan. The appearance of the screen, and the number of decisions you must provide, depends on the level of *The Marketing Game!* that you specified in the setup information at the main Setup and Selection Screen. Once you have entered valid values for all of the plan decisions, you can save your Plan file, print a copy of your plan, and request a pro forma statement.

Warning: It is extremely important that you fill in your plan values accurately and completely. It is very important to doublecheck the entries for your decisions before you press the Save button. Although the program checks entries to screen out some clerical errors, it can't read your mind. And a careless error on your part could cost your firm thousands of dollars. So play it safe and doublecheck your work before you save a file!

Creating a New Marketing Plan

When creating a new marketing plan, the edit fields (boxes) for all of the plan decisions will be blank. To select a field to enter a value, click on it with your mouse or press the Tab key until it is highlighted. Then, use the keyboard to enter the values that you want to use for your marketing decisions. Marketing research report decisions are an exception. To indicate that you want a particular marketing research report, click on the check box next to the name of the report. Reports that are checked will be purchased. (If you change your mind, click on the box again and the check will disappear).

Acceptable ranges of values for most edit boxes are listed on the screen or in the hints displayed in the status bar at the bottom of the screen. The program won't allow you to enter a value that is out of range, and if you press a key that is irrelevant to that type of edit field it is ignored.

If you leave a decision field blank or enter invalid values, the field will be highlighted (with the color yellow on most computers). If you see highlighted fields, go back and correct your entries.

If you try to save a plan that has incomplete or invalid values (or try to use it to create a pro forma), the program will provide an error message and you will need to correct the problem before you can proceed.

The online help system provides much more detail on each decision value and also on the button selections that appear on the screen.

Modifying an Existing Marketing Plan

TMGPlan looks in your default directory for a Plan file with the correct name. The file should be named PLANid.TMG, where "id" is your firm ID code (your industry identification letter and firm number). If you specified the wrong default folder, the wrong industry letter identification, or the wrong firm number on the Setup and Selection Screen, TMGPlan will be unable to open your Plan file. In the same vein, you will not be able to open a previously saved Plan file if you don't know the exact password that was used when it was originally saved.

When you open an existing plan, the values for that plan will be displayed on the screen. You can simply modify the values that you wish to change, leaving other values alone.

[Note: It is very important that you specify the correct game level at the Setup and Selection Screen before you open an existing marketing plan. The level value controls which specific decisions you must provide to complete the marketing plan. If you submit a plan at a level lower than what is expected (for example, you submit a Level 1 plan when the president has instructed you to do a Level 2 plan), your Plan file may be missing values for important decisions. In such a case, the president's staff may have no option except to make a guess about what to do. Alternatively, if you submit a plan at a higher level than that specified by your instructor (for example, a Level 2 plan when your instructor specified Level 1), some of your decisions may be ignored and parts of your budget will be wasted. As you can imagine, the president would not take such carelessness lightly.

If, for some reason, the Plan file you want to open was originally created and saved at a higher level than the level you specified on the Setup and Selection Screen, a message box will appear, asking if you want to change the level to the one specified in the file.]

Saving the Plan File

When you are finished entering decisions for your marketing plan, click the Save button to create and save the Plan file. *Until you save your plan*, the work you have done on your marketing plan is temporary. **Whatever values you entered on the screen will be lost if you exit the program or return to the Setup and Selection Screen prior to saving the Plan file.**

When you click the Save button, a password dialog window will appear. To be certain that the password is correctly entered, you will need to type it and then retype it exactly the same way to confirm that it is what you intended. Remember that this is the password that protects the file from unauthorized access so be sure to keep track of it. If you forget it you will have to re-enter your plan from scratch, and you won't be able open the password-protected Report file.

It is worth reiterating a point made earlier. Each time you save a Plan file the program overwrites any previously saved Plan file that is in the default folder and replaces it with a file that is based on the values currently shown on the screen. On the other hand, if you try to save a plan but the save is not successful (for example, if you see a message that says that you need to finish entering or correct values before the plan can be saved), then the Plan file that exists in the default folder is the old one.

Creating a Pro Forma Based on Plan Decisions

Once you have correctly entered the decision values for a plan, you can press the ProForma button if you want a Pro Forma Financial Summary computed based on the plan values you have entered. It is a good idea to request and study the pro forma. Along with other calculations, the pro forma shows what expenses would be charged against your marketing budget with the current marketing plan. Clearly, you want to be certain that you are not planning a strategy that exceeds your available money. The pro forma also shows what profit contribution might be expected from your plan—if you achieve the sales volume implied by your production request! Remember, though, that what sales you actually achieve will depend on many factors—so careful forecasting is important to the accuracy of the pro forma.

When you select the ProForma button, the Inputs for Pro Forma Screen will appear. It prompts you for additional inputs that are needed to do the calculations for a pro forma. Specifically, the screen will request information about the levels of the product features from the previous period (needed to compute R&D for product modification costs), what percent of your sales you expect to come from each channel (needed to compute revenue by channel), and how many reps (if any) have been fired since the last period (needed to compute any firing costs). You must confirm that the correct values for these items are entered each time you compute a pro forma. Otherwise, product modification costs, firing costs, and perhaps other estimates will be based on inaccurate data. In other words, the TMGPlan software does not "track" the history of your previous decisions. Once the values are correctly updated, click the ProForma button and the Pro Forma Financial Estimates will be displayed.

View Reports Screen

At the end of each decision period, you will receive reports from the president of your firm. These reports provide feedback concerning the results that your plan has produced in the market. These will include your financial summary, some general reports, and any marketing research reports you requested. These may come to you in printed form; however, if a report is provided electronically (i.e., in a computer file), the View Reports Screen is where you can decrypt the form (if necessary), view it, print it, and/or save it in a standard text file format.

Here's a step-by-step overview of how to work with a report that is given to you in electronic form.

The file will be named REPORTid.TMG (where "id" is your firm ID code – your industry letter and firm number) if the Report file is password protected. The file will be named "REPORTid.TXT if it is not password protected. Copy the file to your default TMG folder.

If your default drive for TMG files is a drive with removable disks, insert the disk containing the TMG files before starting the program. Then, start the TMGPlan program.

On the first screen (Setup and Selection Screen), check the industry identification letter, firm number, and game level to ensure that they are correct. Change them if necessary.

Click the "Review or print a report" button. Select the Report file from the open dialog box that will appear.

If the file is password protected, enter the password when prompted to do so. The password is the same one you entered when saving the original Plan file.

The report will be displayed in the File Viewer window. You can browse through the report on screen and/or search for specific text by using on-screen buttons or the menu bar. To print the report, click the Print button. When the print dialog box opens, you will have an opportunity to select which printer to use (if you have more than one printer setup on your computer).

If you wish to save a password-protected file in a text file format (that is, without any encryption or password protection, click the Save button. Specify a different folder and file name in the save dialog box that appears.

The TMGftp Program

The firm has developed a program, TMGftp, that makes it easy to submit Plan files and retrieve encrypted report files over the Internet or the organization's computer network. That's all it does, but sometimes that's a very convenient capability.

Like the TMGPlan program, TMGftp has a complete online help system so there's not a need to go into much detail here. If the president decides that he wants you to use this program, you'll receive additional instructions. However, a few brief points about this easy-to-use software are in order.

First, this program is for use only on computers that have Windows 95 or higher and that have Internet (or network) access. if you use the program on a computer that requires that you do something special to get access to the Internet (for example, if it uses a modem, dialup networking, and a connection to an Internet Service provider to surf the web or use email), do what you normally do to connect to the Internet BEFORE you start the program.

When you start the program, it may take a few seconds for it to load. When the main screen appears there will not be much on it, except edit fields for you to enter your TMG Industry letter and Firm number. Enter those and select the Ok button. Other buttons and information will then appear on the screen.

The appearance of the screen depends on whether or not a configuration file has been automatically loaded by the program. The president will provide a configuration file if you need it.

Sometimes the screen will show edit fields for you to enter information that may be needed to transfer your files (for example, a user log-on name and password). You will receive instructions from the president about how to fill out these fields if they appear. In most cases, however, they will not appear.

The next step is to check to see that the Internet online indicator is green. If it is, you can click the button labeled Connect to FTP host computer. The indicator beside the button will turn green if a connection is established, and at the same time an upload button, a download button, or both will appear on the screen.

Then, all you do is select the upload or download button. A file selection dialog will open for you to select the Plan file to upload, or in the case of a download the folder/directory where you want to save the downloaded report file.

After you have transferred a file, click the button to print or save the session report. It includes a verification number and time stamp that confirms that you submitted your plan and that it is ready and waiting for the president to use it. You should save a copy of this report so that it is available if the president asks you to confirm that the plan was uploaded and on a timely basis.

When you're through, click the Exit button. That's all there is too it.

If there is a problem of some sort with the Internet connection or the connection to the remote (host) computer, you will receive messages and/or the session report may provide diagnostic information. For example, if the remote computer is "down" you won't be able to transfer a file. In a case like that, you may just need to try again later. In any event, it makes seen to check the session report if you have any problems.

Conclusion

This appendix provides information to help you get started with the TMGPlan program. It doesn't cover every detail because the online help system is available and provides more detail if and when you need it. And you will find that using the software is quick and easy.

The TMGPlan program is a simple tool that is designed to do a few specific jobs. It is very easy to use. Yet, some jobs—like viewing a password-protected report or creating an electronic version of your marketing plan decisions—can't be done in any other way. TMGPlan also helps with quality control (checking for invalid or incomplete Plan files), with some utility functions (like printing reports), and calculations (by creating a pro forma for a specific plan).

On the other hand, the TMGPlan software is just a support tool. It does not make marketing plan decisions for you and it can't determine if a plan that you have created is the best one possible (or even a sensible one!). It does not interpret the results of reports that are returned to you and it doesn't draw conclusions about what you should do next. You are the marketing manager, and these jobs are your responsibility.

The appendix also briefly introduces the TMGftp program. The president has not yet decided how he would like for you to submit your marketing plan. However, if he decides that he wants you to use the TMGftp program to submit the electronic version of your plan (that is, the Plan file produced with the TMGPlan software), you will receive addition instructions concerning the TMGftp program.

As a closing note, those of us in the IT department would like to wish you success with your new marketing management responsibilities. After all, if our firm doesn't do a great job meeting the needs of customers we'll all be looking for new jobs!

Index

Forms

Copies of the various forms discussed earlier in this manual are provided on the following pages. Specifically, you will find:

- 10 copies of the Level 1 Marketing Plan Decisions Form
- 10 copies of the Level 2 Marketing Plan Decisions Form
- 10 copies of the Level 3 Marketing Plan Decisions Form
- 10 copies of the Budget Planning Form (front) and Strategy Summary Form (back).

The president will let you know if you are required to turn in a completed copy of one or more of these forms. However, keeping a completed copy of the relevant form for each plan period can be useful to you in reviewing changes in your plan over time.

Marketing Plan Decisions Form – Level 1

Marketing Plan Decisions - Level 1

General

Channel 1	Channel 2	
40	20	Distribution intensity (% of dealers)
13	7	Number of sales reps (0-100)

125,000 Customer service budget
($0-$9,999,999)

Marketing Research

Product 1

1. Share by segment ☐
2. Share by channel ☐
   3. Preferences ☑
   4. Effectiveness ☑
5. Segment by channel ☐
   6. Shopping habits ☐

Industry and Firm

B 4

Product 1

AJVRD Brand name (8 letters)

Features
- 10 Special Commands (5-20)
- 6 Error Protection (1-10)
- 5 Ease of Learning (1-10)

25,000 Production Order Quantity (> 99)

300,000 Advertising Spending

127.16
Wholesale Price
($75-$250)

Marketing Plan Decisions Form – Level 2

Marketing Plan Decisions - Level 2

General

Channel 1   Channel 2

☐	☐	Distribution intensity (% of dealers)
☐	☐	Number of sales reps (0-100)
☐	☐	Percent non-selling time (0-50%)
☐		Sales commission percent (5-15%)
☐		Customer service budget ($0-$9,999,999)

Marketing Research

Product 1

1. Share by segment ☐
2. Share by channel ☐
3. Preferences ☐
4. Effectiveness ☐
5. Segment by channel ☐
6. Shopping habits ☐
7. Product positioning ☐

Industry and Firm

☐ ☐

Product 1

☐	Brand name (8 letters)

Features
- ☐ Special Commands (5-20)
- ☐ Error Protection (1-10)
- ☐ Ease of Learning (1-10)

☐	Production Order Quantity (> 99)
☐	Advertising Spending
☐	Type of Advertising (P,D,I,R, or C)

Channel 1   Channel 2

☐	☐	Sales Promotion
☐	☐	Wholesale Price ($75-$250)

Marketing Plan Decisions Form - Level 3

Marketing Plan Decisions - Level 3 -

General

Channel 1	Channel 2	
☐	☐	Distribution intensity (% of dealers)
☐	☐	Number of sales reps (0-100)
☐	☐	Percent non-selling time (0-50%)
☐		Sales commission percent (5-15%)
☐		Customer service budget ($0-$9,999,999)

Marketing Research

	Product 1	Product 2
1. Share by segment	☐	☐ 1.
2. Share by channel	☐	☐ 2.
3. Preferences	☐	☐ 3.
4. Effectiveness	☐	☐ 4.
5. Segment by channel	☐	☐ 5.
6. Shopping habits	☐	
7. Product positioning	☐	☐ 7.

Industry and Firm

☐ ☐

☐ Click if you have a second product

Product 1

☐	Brand name (8 letters)
Features ☐	Special Commands (5-20)
☐	Error Protection (1-10)
☐	Ease of Learning (1-10)
☐	Production Order Quantity (> 99)
☐	Advertising Spending
☐	Type of Advertising (P,D,I,R, or C)

Channel 1	Channel 2	
☐	☐	Sales Promotion
☐	☐	Wholesale Price ($75-$250)

Product 2

☐	Brand name (8 letters)
Features ☐	Number of tasks (1-10)
☐	Similarity of commands (1-10)
☐	Ability to customize (1-10)
☐	Production Order Quantity (>0)
☐	Advertising Spending
☐	Type of Advertising (P,D,I,R, or C)

Channel 1	Channel 2	
☐	☐	Sales Promotion
☐	☐	Wholesale Price ($35-$200)

Marketing Budget Planning Form

****** **Financial Summary / Pro Forma** ******

Industry: _____ Firm: _____ Period: _____ Brandname: _____

	Channel 1	Channel 2	Total
(1) Estimated Units Sold	_____	_____	_____
(2) Wholesale Price	$_____	$_____	
(3) Base Unit Cost	$_____	$_____	
(4) Gross Sales [(1) x (2)]	$_____	$_____	$_____
(5) Cost of Goods Sold [(1) x (3)]	$_____	$_____	$_____
(6) GROSS MARGIN [(4) minus (5)]			$_____

EXPENSES:

	Channel 1	Channel 2	Total
(7) Advertising			$_____
(8) Sales Force-Salary	$_____	$_____	$_____
(9) Sales Force-FiringCosts	$_____	$_____	$_____
(10) Sales Force-Commission	$_____	$_____	$_____
(11) Customer Service			$_____
(12) Sales Promotion	$_____	$_____	$_____
(13) R&D for Product Modification			$_____
(14) Marketing Research			$_____
(15) TOTAL EXPENSES [sum of (7) to (14)]			$_____
(16) Net Contribution to Profit or Loss [(6) minus (15)]			$_____
(17) Total Spending against Budget [(15) minus (10)]			$_____

Marketing Strategy Summary Form

Industry: _____   Firm: _____   Period _____

Target Market:

Product:

Place:

Promotion:

Price:

Competition:

Marketing Plan Decisions Form – Level 1

Marketing Plan Decisions - Level 1

General

Channel 1 Channel 2

[ ] [ ] Distribution intensity (% of dealers)

[ ] [ ] Number of sales reps (0-100)

[ ] Customer service budget
($0-$9,999,999)

Marketing Research

Product 1

1. Share by segment [ ]
2. Share by channel [ ]
3. Preferences [ ]
4. Effectiveness [ ]
5. Segment by channel [ ]
6. Shopping habits [ ]

Industry and Firm

[ ] [ ]

Product 1

[ ] Brand name (8 letters)

Features:
[ ] Special Commands (5-20)
[ ] Error Protection (1-10)
[ ] Ease of Learning (1-10)

[ ] Production Order Quantity (> 99)

[ ] Advertising Spending

[ ] Wholesale Price
($75-$250)

Marketing Plan Decisions Form – Level 2

Marketing Plan Decisions - Level 2

General

Channel 1   Channel 2

☐ ☐ Distribution intensity (% of dealers)

☐ ☐ Number of sales reps (0-100)

☐ ☐ Percent non-selling time (0-50%)

☐ Sales commission percent (5-15%)

☐ Customer service budget
($0-$9,999,999)

Marketing Research

Product 1

1. Share by segment ☐
2. Share by channel ☐
3. Preferences ☐
4. Effectiveness ☐
5. Segment by channel ☐
6. Shopping habits ☐
7. Product positioning ☐

Industry and Firm

☐ ☐

Product 1

☐ Brand name (8 letters)

Features
☐ Special Commands (5-20)
☐ Error Protection (1-10)
☐ Ease of Learning (1-10)

☐ Production Order Quantity (> 99)

☐ Advertising Spending

☐ Type of Advertising (P,D,I,R, or C)

Channel 1   Channel 2

☐ ☐ Sales Promotion

☐ ☐ Wholesale Price
($75-$250)

Marketing Plan Decisions Form - Level 3

Marketing Plan Decisions - Level 3 -

General

Channel 1   Channel 2

- Distribution intensity (% of dealers)
- Number of sales reps (0-100)
- Percent non-selling time (0-50%)
- Sales commission percent (5-15%)
- Customer service budget ($0-$9,999,999)

Marketing Research

	Product 1	Product 2
1. Share by segment	☐	☐ 1.
2. Share by channel	☐	☐ 2.
3. Preferences	☐	☐ 3.
4. Effectiveness	☐	☐ 4.
5. Segment by channel	☐	☐ 5.
6. Shopping habits	☐	
7. Product positioning	☐	☐ 7.

Industry and Firm

☐ Click if you have a second product

Product 1

- Brand name (8 letters)
- Features
  - Special Commands (5-20)
  - Error Protection (1-10)
  - Ease of Learning (1-10)
- Production Order Quantity (> 99)
- Advertising Spending
- Type of Advertising (P,D,I,R, or C)

Channel 1   Channel 2

- Sales Promotion
- Wholesale Price ($75-$250)

Product 2

- Brand name (8 letters)
- Features
  - Number of tasks (1-10)
  - Similarity of commands (1-10)
  - Ability to customize (1-10)
- Production Order Quantity (>0)
- Advertising Spending
- Type of Advertising (P,D,I,R, or C)

Channel 1   Channel 2

- Sales Promotion
- Wholesale Price ($35-$200)

Marketing Budget Planning Form

****** Financial Summary / Pro Forma ******

Industry: _____ Firm: _____ Period: _____ Brandname: _____

	Channel 1	Channel 2	Total
(1) Estimated Units Sold	_____	_____	_____
(2) Wholesale Price	$_____	$_____	
(3) Base Unit Cost	$_____	$_____	
(4) Gross Sales [(1) x (2)]	$_____	$_____	$_____
(5) Cost of Goods Sold [(1) x (3)]	$_____	$_____	$_____
(6) GROSS MARGIN [(4) minus (5)]			$_____

EXPENSES:

	Channel 1	Channel 2	Total
(7) Advertising			$_____
(8) Sales Force-Salary	$_____	$_____	$_____
(9) Sales Force-FiringCosts	$_____	$_____	$_____
(10) Sales Force-Commission	$_____	$_____	$_____
(11) Customer Service			$_____
(12) Sales Promotion	$_____	$_____	$_____
(13) R&D for Product Modification			$_____
(14) Marketing Research			$_____
(15) TOTAL EXPENSES [sum of (7) to (14)]			$_____
(16) Net Contribution to Profit or Loss [(6) minus (15)]			$_____
(17) Total Spending against Budget [(15) minus (10)]			$_____

Marketing Strategy Summary Form

Industry: _____   Firm: _____   Period _____

Target Market:

Product:

Place:

Promotion:

Price:

Competition:

Marketing Plan Decisions Form – Level 1

Marketing Plan Decisions - Level 1

General

Channel 1   Channel 2

[ ]   [ ]   Distribution intensity (% of dealers)

[ ]   [ ]   Number of sales reps (0-100)

[   ]   Customer service budget ($0-$9,999,999)

Marketing Research

Product 1

1. Share by segment [ ]
2. Share by channel [ ]
3. Preferences [ ]
4. Effectiveness [ ]
5. Segment by channel [ ]
6. Shopping habits [ ]

Industry and Firm

[ ] [ ]

Product 1

[   ] Brand name (8 letters)

Features
[ ] Special Commands (5-20)
[ ] Error Protection (1-10)
[ ] Ease of Learning (1-10)

[   ] Production Order Quantity (> 99)

[   ] Advertising Spending

[   ] Wholesale Price ($75-$250)

Marketing Plan Decisions Form – Level 2

Marketing Plan Decisions - Level 2

General

Channel 1   Channel 2

[ ] [ ]   Distribution intensity (% of dealers)

[ ] [ ]   Number of sales reps (0-100)

[ ] [ ]   Percent non-selling time (0-50%)

[ ]   Sales commission percent (5-15%)

[ ]   Customer service budget ($0-$9,999,999)

Marketing Research

Product 1

1. Share by segment [ ]
2. Share by channel [ ]
3. Preferences [ ]
4. Effectiveness [ ]
5. Segment by channel [ ]
6. Shopping habits [ ]
7. Product positioning [ ]

Industry and Firm

[ ] [ ]

Product 1

[ ]   Brand name (8 letters)

Features
[ ]   Special Commands (5-20)
[ ]   Error Protection (1-10)
[ ]   Ease of Learning (1-10)

[ ]   Production Order Quantity (> 99)

[ ]   Advertising Spending

[ ]   Type of Advertising (P,D,I,R, or C)

Channel 1   Channel 2

[ ] [ ]   Sales Promotion

[ ] [ ]   Wholesale Price ($75-$250)

Marketing Plan Decisions Form - Level 3

Marketing Plan Decisions - Level 3 -

General

Channel 1 Channel 2

☐ ☐ Distribution intensity (% of dealers)

☐ ☐ Number of sales reps (0-100)

☐ ☐ Percent non-selling time (0-50%)

☐ Sales commission percent (5-15%)

☐ Customer service budget ($0-$9,999,999)

Marketing Research

	Product 1	Product 2
1. Share by segment	☐	☐ 1.
2. Share by channel	☐	☐ 2.
3. Preferences	☐	☐ 3.
4. Effectiveness	☐	☐ 4.
5. Segment by channel	☐	☐ 5.
6. Shopping habits	☐	
7. Product positioning	☐	☐ 7.

Industry and Firm

☐ ☐

☐ Click if you have a second product

Product 1

☐ Brand name (8 letters)

Features:
☐ Special Commands (5-20)
☐ Error Protection (1-10)
☐ Ease of Learning (1-10)

☐ Production Order Quantity (> 99)

☐ Advertising Spending

☐ Type of Advertising (P,D,I,R, or C)

Channel 1 Channel 2

☐ ☐ Sales Promotion

☐ ☐ Wholesale Price ($75-$250)

Product 2

☐ Brand name (8 letters)

Features:
☐ Number of tasks (1-10)
☐ Similarity of commands (1-10)
☐ Ability to customize (1-10)

☐ Production Order Quantity (>0)

☐ Advertising Spending

☐ Type of Advertising (P,D,I,R, or C)

Channel 1 Channel 2

☐ ☐ Sales Promotion

☐ ☐ Wholesale Price ($35-$200)

Marketing Budget Planning Form

******Financial Summary / Pro Forma ******

Industry: _____ Firm: _____ Period: _____ Brandname: _____

	Channel 1	Channel 2	Total
(1) Estimated Units Sold	_____	_____	_____
(2) Wholesale Price	$_____	$_____	
(3) Base Unit Cost	$_____	$_____	
(4) Gross Sales [(1) x (2)]	$_____	$_____	$_____
(5) Cost of Goods Sold [(1) x (3)]	$_____	$_____	$_____
(6) GROSS MARGIN [(4) minus (5)]			$_____

EXPENSES:

	Channel 1	Channel 2	Total
(7) Advertising			$_____
(8) Sales Force-Salary	$_____	$_____	$_____
(9) Sales Force-FiringCosts	$_____	$_____	$_____
(10) Sales Force-Commission	$_____	$_____	$_____
(11) Customer Service			$_____
(12) Sales Promotion	$_____	$_____	$_____
(13) R&D for Product Modification			$_____
(14) Marketing Research			$_____
(15) TOTAL EXPENSES [sum of (7) to (14)]			$_____
(16) Net Contribution to Profit or Loss [(6) minus (15)]			$_____
(17) Total Spending against Budget [(15) minus (10)]			$_____

Marketing Strategy Summary Form

Industry: _____   Firm: _____   Period _____

Target Market:

Product:

Place:

Promotion:

Price:

Competition:

Marketing Plan Decisions Form – Level 1

Marketing Plan Decisions - Level 1

General

Channel 1   Channel 2

☐   ☐   Distribution intensity (% of dealers)

☐   ☐   Number of sales reps (0-100)

☐   Customer service budget
($0-$9,999,999)

Marketing Research

Product 1

1. Share by segment ☐
2. Share by channel ☐
3. Preferences ☐
4. Effectiveness ☐
5. Segment by channel ☐
6. Shopping habits ☐

Industry and Firm

☐ ☐

Product 1

☐   Brand name (8 letters)

Features   ☐   Special Commands (5-20)

☐   Error Protection (1-10)

☐   Ease of Learning (1-10)

☐   Production Order Quantity (> 99)

☐   Advertising Spending

☐   Wholesale Price
($75-$250)

Marketing Plan Decisions Form – Level 2

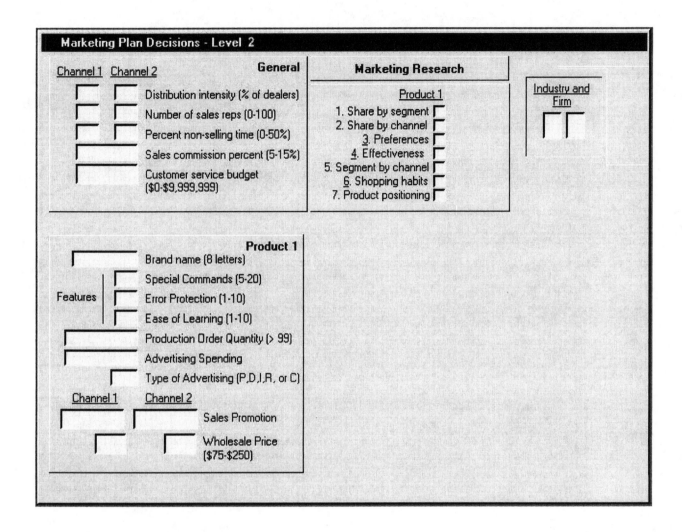

Marketing Plan Decisions Form - Level 3

Marketing Plan Decisions - Level 3 -

General

Channel 1   Channel 2

☐   ☐   Distribution intensity (% of dealers)

☐   ☐   Number of sales reps (0-100)

☐   ☐   Percent non-selling time (0-50%)

☐   Sales commission percent (5-15%)

☐   Customer service budget ($0-$9,999,999)

Marketing Research

	Product 1	Product 2
1. Share by segment	☐	☐ 1.
2. Share by channel	☐	☐ 2.
3. Preferences	☐	☐ 3.
4. Effectiveness	☐	☐ 4.
5. Segment by channel	☐	☐ 5.
6. Shopping habits	☐	
7. Product positioning	☐	☐ 7.

Industry and Firm

☐   ☐

☐ Click if you have a second product

Product 1

☐   Brand name (8 letters)

Features   ☐   Special Commands (5-20)

☐   Error Protection (1-10)

☐   Ease of Learning (1-10)

☐   Production Order Quantity (> 99)

☐   Advertising Spending

☐   Type of Advertising (P,D,I,R, or C)

Channel 1   Channel 2

☐   ☐   Sales Promotion

☐   ☐   Wholesale Price ($75-$250)

Product 2

☐   Brand name (8 letters)

Features   ☐   Number of tasks (1-10)

☐   Similarity of commands (1-10)

☐   Ability to customize (1-10)

☐   Production Order Quantity (>0)

☐   Advertising Spending

☐   Type of Advertising (P,D,I,R, or C)

Channel 1   Channel 2

☐   ☐   Sales Promotion

☐   ☐   Wholesale Price ($35-$200)

Marketing Budget Planning Form

******Financial Summary / Pro Forma ******

Industry: _____ Firm: _____ Period: _____ Brandname: _____

	Channel 1	Channel 2	Total
(1) Estimated Units Sold	_____	_____	_____
(2) Wholesale Price	$_____	$_____	
(3) Base Unit Cost	$_____	$_____	
(4) Gross Sales [(1) x (2)]	$_____	$_____	$_____
(5) Cost of Goods Sold [(1) x (3)]	$_____	$_____	$_____
(6) GROSS MARGIN [(4) minus (5)]			$_____

EXPENSES:

	Channel 1	Channel 2	Total
(7) Advertising			$_____
(8) Sales Force-Salary	$_____	$_____	$_____
(9) Sales Force-FiringCosts	$_____	$_____	$_____
(10) Sales Force-Commission	$_____	$_____	$_____
(11) Customer Service			$_____
(12) Sales Promotion	$_____	$_____	$_____
(13) R&D for Product Modification			$_____
(14) Marketing Research			$_____
(15) TOTAL EXPENSES [sum of (7) to (14)]			$_____
(16) Net Contribution to Profit or Loss [(6) minus (15)]			$_____
(17) Total Spending against Budget [(15) minus (10)]			$_____

Marketing Strategy Summary Form

Industry: _____   Firm: _____   Period _____

Target Market:

Product:

Place:

Promotion:

Price:

Competition:

Marketing Plan Decisions Form – Level 1

Marketing Plan Decisions - Level 1

General

Channel 1 Channel 2

☐ ☐ Distribution intensity (% of dealers)

☐ ☐ Number of sales reps (0-100)

☐ Customer service budget
($0-$9,999,999)

Marketing Research

Product 1

1. Share by segment ☐
2. Share by channel ☐
3. Preferences ☐
4. Effectiveness ☐
5. Segment by channel ☐
6. Shopping habits ☐

Industry and Firm

☐ ☐

Product 1

☐ Brand name (8 letters)

Features
☐ Special Commands (5-20)
☐ Error Protection (1-10)
☐ Ease of Learning (1-10)

☐ Production Order Quantity (> 99)

☐ Advertising Spending

☐ Wholesale Price
($75-$250)

Marketing Plan Decisions Form – Level 2

Marketing Plan Decisions - Level 2

General

Channel 1   **Channel 2**

[ ]	[ ]	Distribution intensity (% of dealers)
[ ]	[ ]	Number of sales reps (0-100)
[ ]	[ ]	Percent non-selling time (0-50%)
[ ]		Sales commission percent (5-15%)
[ ]		Customer service budget ($0-$9,999,999)

Marketing Research

Product 1

1. Share by segment [ ]
2. Share by channel [ ]
3. Preferences [ ]
4. Effectiveness [ ]
5. Segment by channel [ ]
6. Shopping habits [ ]
7. Product positioning [ ]

Industry and Firm

[ ] [ ]

Product 1

[ ] Brand name (8 letters)

Features
- [ ] Special Commands (5-20)
- [ ] Error Protection (1-10)
- [ ] Ease of Learning (1-10)

[ ] Production Order Quantity (> 99)

[ ] Advertising Spending

[ ] Type of Advertising (P,D,I,R, or C)

Channel 1   **Channel 2**

[ ]	[ ]	Sales Promotion
[ ]	[ ]	Wholesale Price ($75-$250)

Marketing Plan Decisions Form - Level 3

Marketing Plan Decisions - Level 3 -

General

Channel 1   Channel 2

- Distribution intensity (% of dealers)
- Number of sales reps (0-100)
- Percent non-selling time (0-50%)
- Sales commission percent (5-15%)
- Customer service budget ($0-$9,999,999)

Marketing Research

	Product 1	Product 2
1. Share by segment	☐	☐ 1.
2. Share by channel	☐	☐ 2.
3. Preferences	☐	☐ 3.
4. Effectiveness	☐	☐ 4.
5. Segment by channel	☐	☐ 5.
6. Shopping habits	☐	
7. Product positioning	☐	☐ 7.

Industry and Firm

☐ Click if you have a second product

Product 1

- Brand name (8 letters)
- Features
  - Special Commands (5-20)
  - Error Protection (1-10)
  - Ease of Learning (1-10)
- Production Order Quantity (> 99)
- Advertising Spending
- Type of Advertising (P,D,I,R, or C)

Channel 1   Channel 2

- Sales Promotion
- Wholesale Price ($75-$250)

Product 2

- Brand name (8 letters)
- Features
  - Number of tasks (1-10)
  - Similarity of commands (1-10)
  - Ability to customize (1-10)
- Production Order Quantity (>0)
- Advertising Spending
- Type of Advertising (P,D,I,R, or C)

Channel 1   Channel 2

- Sales Promotion
- Wholesale Price ($35-$200)

Marketing Budget Planning Form

****** Financial Summary / Pro Forma ******

Industry: _____ Firm: _____ Period: _____ Brandname: _____

	Channel 1	Channel 2	Total
(1) Estimated Units Sold	_____	_____	_____
(2) Wholesale Price	$_____	$_____	
(3) Base Unit Cost	$_____	$_____	
(4) Gross Sales [(1) x (2)]	$_____	$_____	$_____
(5) Cost of Goods Sold [(1) x (3)]	$_____	$_____	$_____
(6) GROSS MARGIN [(4) minus (5)]			$_____

EXPENSES:

	Channel 1	Channel 2	Total
(7) Advertising			$_____
(8) Sales Force-Salary	$_____	$_____	$_____
(9) Sales Force-FiringCosts	$_____	$_____	$_____
(10) Sales Force-Commission	$_____	$_____	$_____
(11) Customer Service			$_____
(12) Sales Promotion	$_____	$_____	$_____
(13) R&D for Product Modification			$_____
(14) Marketing Research			$_____
(15) TOTAL EXPENSES [sum of (7) to (14)]			$_____
(16) Net Contribution to Profit or Loss [(6) minus (15)]			$_____
(17) Total Spending against Budget [(15) minus (10)]			$_____

Marketing Strategy Summary Form

Industry: _____   Firm: _____   Period _____

Target Market:

Product:

Place:

Promotion:

Price:

Competition:

Marketing Plan Decisions Form – Level 1

Marketing Plan Decisions - Level 1

General

Channel 1   Channel 2

☐ ☐ Distribution intensity (% of dealers)

☐ ☐ Number of sales reps (0-100)

☐ Customer service budget
($0-$9,999,999)

Marketing Research

Product 1

1. Share by segment ☐
2. Share by channel ☐
3. Preferences ☐
4. Effectiveness ☐
5. Segment by channel ☐
6. Shopping habits ☐

Industry and Firm

☐ ☐

Product 1

☐ Brand name (8 letters)

Features
☐ Special Commands (5-20)
☐ Error Protection (1-10)
☐ Ease of Learning (1-10)

☐ Production Order Quantity (> 99)

☐ Advertising Spending

☐ Wholesale Price
($75-$250)

Marketing Plan Decisions Form – Level 2

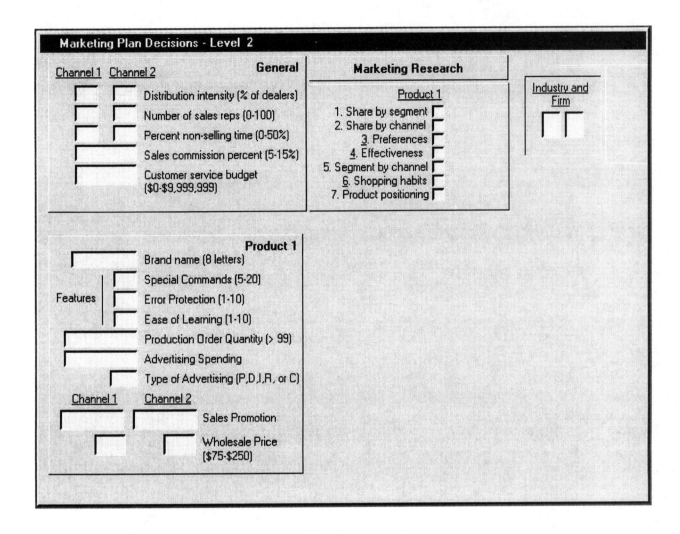

Marketing Plan Decisions Form - Level 3

Marketing Plan Decisions - Level 3 -

General

Channel 1 Channel 2

[ ]	[ ]	Distribution intensity (% of dealers)
[ ]	[ ]	Number of sales reps (0-100)
[ ]	[ ]	Percent non-selling time (0-50%)
[ ]		Sales commission percent (5-15%)
[ ]		Customer service budget ($0-$9,999,999)

Marketing Research

	Product 1	Product 2
1. Share by segment	[ ]	[ ] 1.
2. Share by channel	[ ]	[ ] 2.
3. Preferences	[ ]	[ ] 3.
4. Effectiveness	[ ]	[ ] 4.
5. Segment by channel	[ ]	[ ] 5.
6. Shopping habits	[ ]	
7. Product positioning	[ ]	[ ] 7.

Industry and Firm

[ ] [ ]

[ ] Click if you have a second product

Product 1

[ ]	Brand name (8 letters)
Features [ ]	Special Commands (5-20)
[ ]	Error Protection (1-10)
[ ]	Ease of Learning (1-10)
[ ]	Production Order Quantity (> 99)
[ ]	Advertising Spending
[ ]	Type of Advertising (P,D,I,R, or C)

Channel 1 Channel 2

[ ]	[ ]	Sales Promotion
[ ]	[ ]	Wholesale Price ($75-$250)

Product 2

[ ]	Brand name (8 letters)
Features [ ]	Number of tasks (1-10)
[ ]	Similarity of commands (1-10)
[ ]	Ability to customize (1-10)
[ ]	Production Order Quantity (>0)
[ ]	Advertising Spending
[ ]	Type of Advertising (P,D,I,R, or C)

Channel 1 Channel 2

[ ]	[ ]	Sales Promotion
[ ]	[ ]	Wholesale Price ($35-$200)

Marketing Budget Planning Form

****** Financial Summary / Pro Forma ******

Industry: _____ Firm: _____ Period: _____ Brandname: _____

	Channel 1	Channel 2	Total
(1) Estimated Units Sold	_____	_____	_____
(2) Wholesale Price	$_____	$_____	
(3) Base Unit Cost	$_____	$_____	
(4) Gross Sales [(1) x (2)]	$_____	$_____	$_____
(5) Cost of Goods Sold [(1) x (3)]	$_____	$_____	$_____
(6) GROSS MARGIN [(4) minus (5)]			$_____

EXPENSES:

	Channel 1	Channel 2	Total
(7) Advertising			$_____
(8) Sales Force-Salary	$_____	$_____	$_____
(9) Sales Force-FiringCosts	$_____	$_____	$_____
(10) Sales Force-Commission	$_____	$_____	$_____
(11) Customer Service			$_____
(12) Sales Promotion	$_____	$_____	$_____
(13) R&D for Product Modification			$_____
(14) Marketing Research			$_____
(15) TOTAL EXPENSES [sum of (7) to (14)]			$_____
(16) Net Contribution to Profit or Loss [(6) minus (15)]			$_____
(17) Total Spending against Budget [(15) minus (10)]			$_____

Marketing Strategy Summary Form

Industry: _____   Firm: _____   Period _____

Target Market:

Product:

Place:

Promotion:

Price:

Competition:

Marketing Plan Decisions Form – Level 1

Marketing Plan Decisions - Level 1

General

Channel 1   Channel 2

☐   ☐   Distribution intensity (% of dealers)

☐   ☐   Number of sales reps (0-100)

☐   Customer service budget ($0-$9,999,999)

Marketing Research

Product 1

1. Share by segment ☐
2. Share by channel ☐
3. Preferences ☐
4. Effectiveness ☐
5. Segment by channel ☐
6. Shopping habits ☐

Industry and Firm

☐ ☐

Product 1

☐   Brand name (8 letters)

Features ☐   Special Commands (5-20)

☐   Error Protection (1-10)

☐   Ease of Learning (1-10)

☐   Production Order Quantity (> 99)

☐   Advertising Spending

☐   Wholesale Price ($75-$250)

Marketing Plan Decisions Form – Level 2

Marketing Plan Decisions - Level 2

General

Channel 1 | **Channel 2**

- [ ] [ ] Distribution intensity (% of dealers)
- [ ] [ ] Number of sales reps (0-100)
- [ ] [ ] Percent non-selling time (0-50%)
- [ ] Sales commission percent (5-15%)
- [ ] Customer service budget ($0-$9,999,999)

Marketing Research

Product 1

1. Share by segment [ ]
2. Share by channel [ ]
3. Preferences [ ]
4. Effectiveness [ ]
5. Segment by channel [ ]
6. Shopping habits [ ]
7. Product positioning [ ]

Industry and Firm

[ ] [ ]

Product 1

- [ ] Brand name (8 letters)

Features
- [ ] Special Commands (5-20)
- [ ] Error Protection (1-10)
- [ ] Ease of Learning (1-10)
- [ ] Production Order Quantity (> 99)
- [ ] Advertising Spending
- [ ] Type of Advertising (P,D,I,R, or C)

Channel 1 | **Channel 2**

- [ ] [ ] Sales Promotion
- [ ] [ ] Wholesale Price ($75-$250)

Marketing Plan Decisions Form - Level 3

Marketing Plan Decisions - Level 3 -

General

Channel 1   Channel 2

- Distribution intensity (% of dealers)
- Number of sales reps (0-100)
- Percent non-selling time (0-50%)
- Sales commission percent (5-15%)
- Customer service budget ($0-$9,999,999)

Marketing Research

	Product 1	Product 2
1. Share by segment		1.
2. Share by channel		2.
3. Preferences		3.
4. Effectiveness		4.
5. Segment by channel		5.
6. Shopping habits		
7. Product positioning		7.

Industry and Firm

☐ Click if you have a second product

Product 1

- Brand name (8 letters)

Features
- Special Commands (5-20)
- Error Protection (1-10)
- Ease of Learning (1-10)
- Production Order Quantity (> 99)
- Advertising Spending
- Type of Advertising (P,D,I,R, or C)

Channel 1   Channel 2
- Sales Promotion
- Wholesale Price ($75-$250)

Product 2

- Brand name (8 letters)

Features
- Number of tasks (1-10)
- Similarity of commands (1-10)
- Ability to customize (1-10)
- Production Order Quantity (>0)
- Advertising Spending
- Type of Advertising (P,D,I,R, or C)

Channel 1   Channel 2
- Sales Promotion
- Wholesale Price ($35-$200)

Marketing Budget Planning Form

******Financial Summary / Pro Forma ******

Industry: _____   Firm: _____   Period: _____   Brandname: _____

	Channel 1	Channel 2	Total
(1) Estimated Units Sold	_____	_____	_____
(2) Wholesale Price	$_____	$_____	
(3) Base Unit Cost	$_____	$_____	
(4) Gross Sales [(1) x (2)]	$_____	$_____	$_____
(5) Cost of Goods Sold [(1) x (3)]	$_____	$_____	$_____
(6) GROSS MARGIN [(4) minus (5)]			$_____

EXPENSES:

	Channel 1	Channel 2	Total
(7) Advertising			$_____
(8) Sales Force-Salary	$_____	$_____	$_____
(9) Sales Force-FiringCosts	$_____	$_____	$_____
(10) Sales Force-Commission	$_____	$_____	$_____
(11) Customer Service			$_____
(12) Sales Promotion	$_____	$_____	$_____
(13) R&D for Product Modification			$_____
(14) Marketing Research			$_____
(15) TOTAL EXPENSES [sum of (7) to (14)]			$_____
(16) Net Contribution to Profit or Loss [(6) minus (15)]			$_____
(17) Total Spending against Budget [(15) minus (10)]			$_____

Marketing Strategy Summary Form

Industry: _____   Firm: _____   Period _____

Target Market:

Product:

Place:

Promotion:

Price:

Competition:

Marketing Plan Decisions Form – Level 1

Marketing Plan Decisions - Level 1

General

Channel 1 Channel 2

[ ] [ ] Distribution intensity (% of dealers)

[ ] [ ] Number of sales reps (0-100)

[ ] Customer service budget
($0-$9,999,999)

Marketing Research

Product 1

1. Share by segment [ ]
2. Share by channel [ ]
3. Preferences [ ]
4. Effectiveness [ ]
5. Segment by channel [ ]
6. Shopping habits [ ]

Industry and Firm

[ ] [ ]

Product 1

[ ] Brand name (8 letters)

Features
[ ] Special Commands (5-20)
[ ] Error Protection (1-10)
[ ] Ease of Learning (1-10)

[ ] Production Order Quantity (> 99)

[ ] Advertising Spending

[ ] Wholesale Price
($75-$250)

Marketing Plan Decisions Form – Level 2

Marketing Plan Decisions - Level 2

General

Channel 1	Channel 2	
☐	☐	Distribution intensity (% of dealers)
☐	☐	Number of sales reps (0-100)
☐	☐	Percent non-selling time (0-50%)
☐		Sales commission percent (5-15%)
☐		Customer service budget ($0-$9,999,999)

Marketing Research

Product 1

1. Share by segment ☐
2. Share by channel ☐
3. Preferences ☐
4. Effectiveness ☐
5. Segment by channel ☐
6. Shopping habits ☐
7. Product positioning ☐

Industry and Firm

☐ ☐

Product 1

☐	Brand name (8 letters)
Features ☐	Special Commands (5-20)
☐	Error Protection (1-10)
☐	Ease of Learning (1-10)
☐	Production Order Quantity (> 99)
☐	Advertising Spending
☐	Type of Advertising (P,D,I,R, or C)

Channel 1	Channel 2	
☐	☐	Sales Promotion
☐	☐	Wholesale Price ($75-$250)

Marketing Plan Decisions Form - Level 3

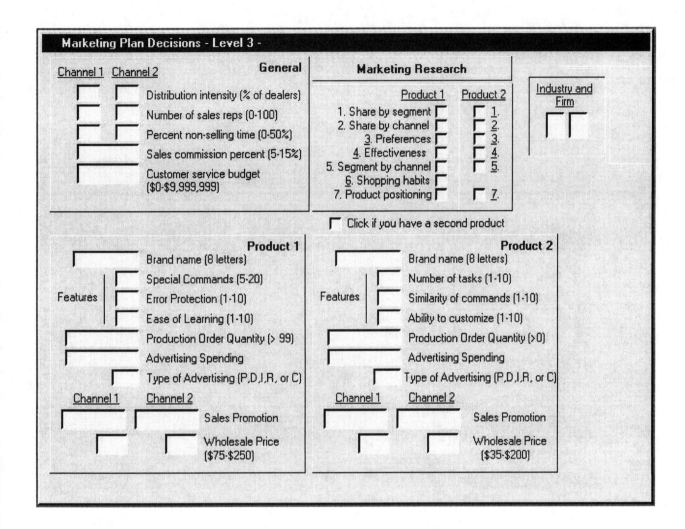

Marketing Budget Planning Form

******Financial Summary / Pro Forma ******

Industry: _____ Firm: _____ Period: _____ Brandname: _____

	Channel 1	Channel 2	Total
(1) Estimated Units Sold	_____	_____	_____
(2) Wholesale Price	$_____	$_____	
(3) Base Unit Cost	$_____	$_____	
(4) Gross Sales [(1) x (2)]	$_____	$_____	$_____
(5) Cost of Goods Sold [(1) x (3)]	$_____	$_____	$_____
(6) GROSS MARGIN [(4) minus (5)]			$_____

EXPENSES:

	Channel 1	Channel 2	Total
(7) Advertising			$_____
(8) Sales Force-Salary	$_____	$_____	$_____
(9) Sales Force-FiringCosts	$_____	$_____	$_____
(10) Sales Force-Commission	$_____	$_____	$_____
(11) Customer Service			$_____
(12) Sales Promotion	$_____	$_____	$_____
(13) R&D for Product Modification			$_____
(14) Marketing Research			$_____
(15) TOTAL EXPENSES [sum of (7) to (14)]			$_____
(16) Net Contribution to Profit or Loss [(6) minus (15)]			$_____
(17) Total Spending against Budget [(15) minus (10)]			$_____

Marketing Strategy Summary Form

Industry: _____   Firm: _____   Period _____

Target Market:

Product:

Place:

Promotion:

Price:

Competition:

Marketing Plan Decisions Form – Level 1

Marketing Plan Decisions - Level 1

General

Channel 1   Channel 2

[ ]   [ ]   Distribution intensity (% of dealers)
[ ]   [ ]   Number of sales reps (0-100)

[   ]   Customer service budget ($0-$9,999,999)

Marketing Research

Product 1

1. Share by segment [ ]
2. Share by channel [ ]
3. Preferences [ ]
4. Effectiveness [ ]
5. Segment by channel [ ]
6. Shopping habits [ ]

Industry and Firm

[ ] [ ]

Product 1

[   ]   Brand name (8 letters)

Features
[ ]   Special Commands (5-20)
[ ]   Error Protection (1-10)
[ ]   Ease of Learning (1-10)

[   ]   Production Order Quantity (> 99)
[   ]   Advertising Spending

[   ]   Wholesale Price ($75-$250)

Marketing Plan Decisions Form – Level 2

Marketing Plan Decisions - Level 2

General

Channel 1   Channel 2

- Distribution intensity (% of dealers)
- Number of sales reps (0-100)
- Percent non-selling time (0-50%)
- Sales commission percent (5-15%)
- Customer service budget ($0-$9,999,999)

Marketing Research

Product 1

1. Share by segment
2. Share by channel
3. Preferences
4. Effectiveness
5. Segment by channel
6. Shopping habits
7. Product positioning

Industry and Firm

Product 1

- Brand name (8 letters)

Features
- Special Commands (5-20)
- Error Protection (1-10)
- Ease of Learning (1-10)

- Production Order Quantity (> 99)
- Advertising Spending
- Type of Advertising (P,D,I,R, or C)

Channel 1   Channel 2

- Sales Promotion
- Wholesale Price ($75-$250)

Marketing Plan Decisions Form - Level 3

Marketing Plan Decisions - Level 3 -

General

Channel 1	Channel 2	
☐	☐	Distribution intensity (% of dealers)
☐	☐	Number of sales reps (0-100)
☐	☐	Percent non-selling time (0-50%)
☐		Sales commission percent (5-15%)
☐		Customer service budget ($0-$9,999,999)

Marketing Research

	Product 1	Product 2
1. Share by segment	☐	☐ 1.
2. Share by channel	☐	☐ 2.
3. Preferences	☐	☐ 3.
4. Effectiveness	☐	☐ 4.
5. Segment by channel	☐	☐ 5.
6. Shopping habits	☐	
7. Product positioning	☐	☐ 7.

Industry and Firm

☐ ☐

☐ Click if you have a second product

Product 1

☐	Brand name (8 letters)
Features ☐	Special Commands (5-20)
☐	Error Protection (1-10)
☐	Ease of Learning (1-10)
☐	Production Order Quantity (> 99)
☐	Advertising Spending
☐	Type of Advertising (P,D,I,R, or C)

Channel 1	Channel 2	
☐	☐	Sales Promotion
☐	☐	Wholesale Price ($75-$250)

Product 2

☐	Brand name (8 letters)
Features ☐	Number of tasks (1-10)
☐	Similarity of commands (1-10)
☐	Ability to customize (1-10)
☐	Production Order Quantity (>0)
☐	Advertising Spending
☐	Type of Advertising (P,D,I,R, or C)

Channel 1	Channel 2	
☐	☐	Sales Promotion
☐	☐	Wholesale Price ($35-$200)

Marketing Budget Planning Form

******Financial Summary / Pro Forma ******

Industry: _____ Firm: _____ Period: _____ Brandname: _____

	Channel 1	Channel 2	Total
(1) Estimated Units Sold	_____	_____	_____
(2) Wholesale Price	$_____	$_____	
(3) Base Unit Cost	$_____	$_____	
(4) Gross Sales [(1) x (2)]	$_____	$_____	$_____
(5) Cost of Goods Sold [(1) x (3)]	$_____	$_____	$_____
(6) GROSS MARGIN [(4) minus (5)]			$_____

EXPENSES:

	Channel 1	Channel 2	Total
(7) Advertising			$_____
(8) Sales Force-Salary	$_____	$_____	$_____
(9) Sales Force-FiringCosts	$_____	$_____	$_____
(10) Sales Force-Commission	$_____	$_____	$_____
(11) Customer Service			$_____
(12) Sales Promotion	$_____	$_____	$_____
(13) R&D for Product Modification			$_____
(14) Marketing Research			$_____
(15) TOTAL EXPENSES [sum of (7) to (14)]			$_____
(16) Net Contribution to Profit or Loss [(6) minus (15)]			$_____
(17) Total Spending against Budget [(15) minus (10)]			$_____

Marketing Strategy Summary Form

Industry: _____   Firm: _____   Period _____

Target Market:

Product:

Place:

Promotion:

Price:

Competition:

Marketing Plan Decisions Form – Level 1

Marketing Plan Decisions - Level 1

General

Channel 1   Channel 2

☐   ☐   Distribution intensity (% of dealers)

☐   ☐   Number of sales reps (0-100)

☐   Customer service budget ($0-$9,999,999)

Marketing Research

Product 1

1. Share by segment ☐
2. Share by channel ☐
3. Preferences ☐
4. Effectiveness ☐
5. Segment by channel ☐
6. Shopping habits ☐

Industry and Firm

☐ ☐

Product 1

☐ Brand name (8 letters)

Features
- ☐ Special Commands (5-20)
- ☐ Error Protection (1-10)
- ☐ Ease of Learning (1-10)

☐ Production Order Quantity (> 99)

☐ Advertising Spending

☐ Wholesale Price ($75-$250)

Marketing Plan Decisions Form – Level 2

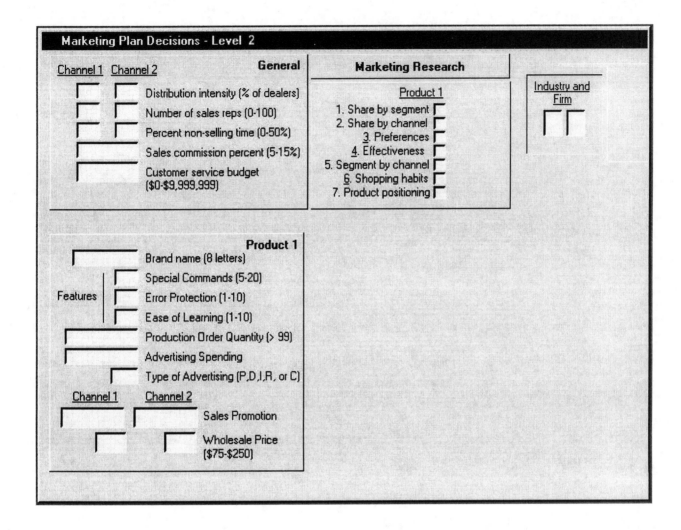

Marketing Plan Decisions Form - Level 3

Marketing Plan Decisions - Level 3 -

General

Channel 1 Channel 2

- Distribution intensity (% of dealers)
- Number of sales reps (0-100)
- Percent non-selling time (0-50%)
- Sales commission percent (5-15%)
- Customer service budget ($0-$9,999,999)

Marketing Research

	Product 1	Product 2
1. Share by segment	☐	☐ 1.
2. Share by channel	☐	☐ 2.
3. Preferences	☐	☐ 3.
4. Effectiveness	☐	☐ 4.
5. Segment by channel	☐	☐ 5.
6. Shopping habits	☐	☐ 6.
7. Product positioning	☐	☐ 7.

Industry and Firm

☐ Click if you have a second product

Product 1

- Brand name (8 letters)
- **Features**
  - Special Commands (5-20)
  - Error Protection (1-10)
  - Ease of Learning (1-10)
- Production Order Quantity (> 99)
- Advertising Spending
- Type of Advertising (P,D,I,R, or C)

Channel 1   Channel 2
- Sales Promotion
- Wholesale Price ($75-$250)

Product 2

- Brand name (8 letters)
- **Features**
  - Number of tasks (1-10)
  - Similarity of commands (1-10)
  - Ability to customize (1-10)
- Production Order Quantity (>0)
- Advertising Spending
- Type of Advertising (P,D,I,R, or C)

Channel 1   Channel 2
- Sales Promotion
- Wholesale Price ($35-$200)

Marketing Budget Planning Form

****** Financial Summary / Pro Forma ******

Industry: _____ Firm: _____ Period: _____ Brandname: _____

	Channel 1	Channel 2	Total
(1) Estimated Units Sold	_____	_____	_____
(2) Wholesale Price	$_____	$_____	
(3) Base Unit Cost	$_____	$_____	
(4) Gross Sales [(1) x (2)]	$_____	$_____	$_____
(5) Cost of Goods Sold [(1) x (3)]	$_____	$_____	$_____
(6) GROSS MARGIN [(4) minus (5)]			$_____

EXPENSES:

	Channel 1	Channel 2	Total
(7) Advertising			$_____
(8) Sales Force-Salary	$_____	$_____	$_____
(9) Sales Force-FiringCosts	$_____	$_____	$_____
(10) Sales Force-Commission	$_____	$_____	$_____
(11) Customer Service			$_____
(12) Sales Promotion	$_____	$_____	$_____
(13) R&D for Product Modification			$_____
(14) Marketing Research			$_____
(15) TOTAL EXPENSES [sum of (7) to (14)]			$_____
(16) Net Contribution to Profit or Loss [(6) minus (15)]			$_____
(17) Total Spending against Budget [(15) minus (10)]			$_____

Marketing Strategy Summary Form

Industry: _____   Firm: _____   Period _____

Target Market:

Product:

Place:

Promotion:

Price:

Competition: